THE TRAGEDY OF
Titus Andronicus

JZtron Papuli.

7/96

D1392397

EDITED BY
George Lyman Kittredge

Revised by Irving Ribner

William Shakespeare

THE TRAGEDY OF

Titus Andronicus

BLAISDELL PUBLISHING COMPANY

A Division of Ginn and Company

WALTHAM, MASSACHUSETTS · TORONTO · LONDON

PREFACE

The New Kittredge Shakespeares

The publication of George Lyman Kittredge's *Complete Works of Shakespeare* in 1936 was a landmark in Shakespeare scholarship. The teacher who for almost half a century had dominated and shaped the direction of Shakespearean study in America produced what was recognized widely as the finest edition of Shakespeare up to his time. In the preface to this edition Kittredge indicated his editorial principles; these allowed a paramount authority to the Folio of 1623 and countenanced few departures from it while, at the same time, refusing to "canonize the heedless type-setters of the Elizabethan printing house." Kittredge's work was marked by a judicious conservatism and a common sense rarely found in equal measure in earlier editors of Shakespeare. In the thirty-odd years which have gone by since the appearance of this monumental volume, however, considerable advances have been made in the establishment of Shakespeare's text, and our body of knowledge about the dates, sources, and general historical background of Shakespeare's plays has vastly increased. The present revision is designed to apply this new knowledge to Kittredge's work so that it may have as much value to the student and general reader of today as it had to those of thirty years ago.

Before his death Kittredge had issued, in addition to *The Complete Works*, separate editions of sixteen of the plays, each copiously annotated. Some of the notes were unusually elaborate, but they interpreted Shakespeare's language with a fullness and precision attained by few other commentators, for Kittredge had few equals in his intimate knowledge of Elizabethan English. In freshly annotating the plays I have, accordingly, tried to use

Kittredge's own notes as fully as space would permit. Where I have repeated his distinctive language or recorded his characteristic critical opinions, I have followed the note with the symbol [κ]; where Kittredge's definition of a term can be found in essentially the same words in other editions, I have not used the identifying symbol. Every annotator draws upon the full body of the notes of earlier editors, and to give credit for every note is impossible. Notes have been placed at page bottoms.

The brief introductions which Kittredge wrote for the plays have been replaced by new ones, for what seemed like indisputable fact some thirty years ago often appears today to be much more uncertain, and many new issues of which Kittredge was not aware have been raised in recent criticism. The new introductions seek to present what are now generally agreed to be basic facts about the plays and to give some indications of the directions which modern criticism has taken, although specific analyses of individual plays are avoided.

Such great authority attaches to Kittredge's text that it has not frequently — and never lightly — been departed from. Where changes have been made, they have usually involved the restoration of copy-text readings now generally accepted in place of the emendations of eighteenth- and nineteenth-century editors of which Kittredge, in spite of his extraordinary conservatism in this regard, sometimes too easily approved. Only rarely has an emendation been adopted in the present revision which was not also adopted by Kittredge. All departures from the copy-texts are indicated in the notes, emendations followed by the names of the editors by whom they were first proposed. Wherever Kittredge's text has been departed from for any reason, his reading is given in the notes. Modern spelling has in a few instances been substituted for Elizabethan forms which are mere spelling variations but which Kittredge nevertheless retained. His punctuation has not been altered except in a few very rare instances.

The system of recording elisions and contractions which Kittredge explained in his introduction to *The Complete Works* has been retained, as has his method of preserving to the fullest the copy-text stage directions, with all additions to them enclosed within square brackets. Although modern editors recognize the vagueness of the place settings of Elizabethan plays and are reluctant to include the place designations so favoured by eighteenth- and nineteenth-century editors, much historical interest nevertheless attaches to these, and Kittredge's place designations accordingly have been retained between square brackets. Kittredge's attempt to retain the line numbering of the Globe text, which resulted in considerable irregularity in prose passages, has been abandoned, and the lines of each play have been freshly numbered. Kittredge's act and scene divisions have been retained, as has his practice of surrounding by square brackets those divisions which are not in the copy-texts.

The plan of *The New Kittredge Shakespeares* is a comprehensive one. They will include a new edition of *The Complete Works* and individual editions of each of the plays, the sonnets, and the poems. A comprehensive introduction to Shakespeare's life, times, and theatrical milieu will be published both as a separate volume and as an introduction to *The Complete Works*.

IRVING RIBNER

INTRODUCTION

The Tragedy of Titus Andronicus

◇◇◇◇◇ Critics traditionally have been reluctant to recognize
◇◇◇◇◇ Shakespeare as the author of *Titus Andronicus,* although
the editors of the First Folio seem to have had no such doubts,
and the play was clearly stated to be Shakespeare's by Francis
Meres in his *Palladis Tamia* of 1598. Philip Henslowe recorded a
performance of a "Titus & Ondronicous" by the Earl of Sussex's
Men on January 24, 1594, marking the play "Ne," his usual manner of indicating a new work. It was entered in the Stationers'
Register by John Danter on February 6, 1594, and issued by him
in quarto in the same year. This edition (Q¹) bore no author's
name on its title page, not an unusual circumstance in the printing of Elizabethan plays, but it did claim that the work had been
"Plaide by the Right Honourable the Earle of Darbie, Earle of
Pembrooke, and Earle of Sussex their Seruants." No one seems to
have questioned Shakespeare's authorship before 1687, when
Edward Ravenscroft wrote in a preface to his own adaptation of
the play that he had been "told by some anciently conversant
with the stage, that it was not Originally his [Shakespeare's], but
brought by a private Author to be Acted, and he only gave some
Master-touches to one or two of the Principal Parts or Characters;
this I am apt to believe, because 'tis the most incorrect and indi-
gested piece in all his works; it seems rather a heap of Rubbish
than a Structure."

Ravenscroft, of course, was primarily interested in advertising
the merits of his own adaptation, but that he may have actually
heard such a rumour is possible. There were countless tales about
Shakespeare current at the end of the seventeenth century which
no one today would accept as genuine. Yet Ravenscroft's denial

of the play to Shakespeare seems to have been more the product of his own critical judgment than of any reliable factual evidence. And it has been such critical judgment — the feeling that *Titus Andronicus* is simply too crude and brutal to have been written by the "gentle" Shakespeare — that has caused many scholars, continuing into our own time, to develop elaborate theories about the play's origins and early theatre history. Some have argued that Shakespeare had no part in it at all, others that he collaborated with one or more of his contemporaries, and still others that his share consisted only of the revision of an older play by one or more earlier writers. Perhaps the most detailed and ingenious argument has been that of John Dover Wilson who, in his New Cambridge edition (Cambridge University Press, 1948), argued that Shakespeare in about the middle of January 1594 revised and augmented a shorter play originally written for a travelling company by George Peele in the summer of 1593. In the revision Wilson holds that Shakespeare may have been assisted by Peele.

These matters probably will never be settled with finality, but there is no piece of evidence for the hand of another author in the play which should be given greater weight than the fact that Heminges and Condell included it in the First Folio as entirely the work of Shakespeare. More and more scholars are coming to believe that they were correct in this. If the play is different from the great tragedies of Shakespeare's maturity, we must recognize that it was almost certainly Shakespeare's first attempt at tragedy and that he was imitating the kind of Senecanism made popular by such contemporary dramatists as Thomas Kyd. There are in *Titus Andronicus,* moreover, elements that are distinctively Shakespearean and which we are to see developed with greater skill in the work of his maturity. Kittredge has perhaps disposed of the authorship controversy most succinctly when he wrote that "Nobody would have listened to Ravenscroft but for the feeling that *Titus Andronicus* is too horrible to be Shakespeare's. But Shakespeare was always prone to try experiments, and it would be strange if he had not written one out-and-out tragedy of blood when Kyd had shown how powerfully such things appealed to playgoers. . . . Distaste for horrors ought not to make one regardless of the skillful construction of the play, of its dramatic power, and of the magnificence of many poetic passages. With all its faults, it is far beyond the abilities of either Peele or Greene. Shakespeare must have the credit as well as the discredit of its authorship."

DATE

Ben Jonson in the Introduction to his *Bartholomew Fair,* printed in 1614, derided *Titus Andronicus,* which he linked with Kyd's *The Spanish Tragedy* (usually dated around 1589), as an outmoded kind of play: "Hee that will sweare, *Ieronimo* [*Spanish Tragedy*], or *Andronicus* are the best plays, yet, shall passe unexcepted at, heere, as a man whose Judgement shews it is constant, and hath stood still, these five and twentie, or thirtie yeares." Although Jonson's round numbers cannot be taken literally, and there is little reason to assume that he knew the exact date of Shakespeare's play in any case, he did link it with a work written before 1590.

We cannot say exactly when *Titus Andronicus* was written. When Henslowe marked it "Ne" in 1594, he may have meant only that he had newly acquired it. It is possible that Shakespeare wrote the play as early as 1589 or 1590, for one of its episodes seems to be referred to in *A Knack to Know A Knave,* which Henslowe reports as acted on June 10 of 1592, and some of the lines of *Titus* seem to be echoed in *The Troublesome Reign of King John,* published in 1591. The unknown author of this work was remarkable for the extent to which he pillaged lines from contemporary plays, and this fact makes it likely that he, rather than Shakespeare, was the borrower. If *Titus Andronicus* was indeed written by Shakespeare before 1590, we must acknowledge that it was the finest work of tragedy written in England up to that time.

TEXT

John Danter's quarto of 1594 (Q¹) was unknown until 1904, when the single extant copy, now in the Folger Library in Washington, D.C., was discovered in Sweden. It is a fairly good text which gives signs of having been printed from Shakespeare's own manuscript (foul papers). Kittredge appears to have been the first editor of Shakespeare to base an edition of the play closely upon it, being followed in this some twelve years later by John Dover Wilson. A second quarto (Q^2) was printed in 1600 from Q^1, with some omissions and corruptions as well as some corrections, and in 1611 a third quarto (Q^3) was printed from Q^2. The text of the play in the folio of 1623 (F^1) was set from a copy of Q^3, but it contains many additional stage directions, some of them showing the hand of a prompter, two additional lines, and one additional whole scene (III.ii.). If the folio editors had access to an independent manuscript, as one might assume from this, it is strange that they should have made no further use of it, and this has been much debated. The best explanation may be that there was no such manuscript, but that F^1 was set from a copy of Q^3 which around 1623 was being used as a theatre promptbook, the scene missing in the quartos probably having been added to it in manuscript along with other changes, and prompter's directions having been inserted where necessary. The F^1 text is divided into five acts, but not into scenes, whereas none of the quartos has act or scene division of any kind. That of the present edition follows the Globe text. All substantive departures from Q^1 are recorded in the notes.

THE SOURCE PROBLEM

The story of Titus Andronicus is one of a group of apocryphal tales about the last days of the Roman Empire which were current in medieval Europe and which, although they contain some quasi-historical elements, have no basis in fact. It is thus extremely unlikely that any such person as the hero of Shakespeare's play ever existed, although the names of some of his characters are borrowed from those of historical persons. An Andronicus Commenus, for instance, was the Emperor of Byzantium from A.D. 1183 to 1185, and his right hand was cut off during the mutilation of his body before he was killed in a popular uprising, but neither he nor the Andronici family to which he belonged have any relation to the characters of Shakespeare's play. The names Bassianus and Saturninus also belonged to historical persons of whom there is record.

How the story came to Shakespeare is uncertain, but the most likely supposition is that his source was a prose *Tragical History of Titus Andronicus*. The source is today extant only in an eighteenth-century reprint of a chapbook which has all the appearances of going back to Shakespeare's time. This chapbook, the single copy of which is now in the Folger Library, contains a ballad about Titus as well as the prose account, and on its title page, which may be a direct transcription of a sixteenth-century one, it reports that the tale is "newly translated from the Italian." Some scholars have held that it was to this prose account rather than to Shakespeare's play that the 1594 Stationers' Register entry referred, and they have used this supposition to argue the earlier date of Shakespeare's play. The ballad seems to have been derived almost entirely from the prose, although it contains some elements which accord with Shakespeare's play rather than with the chapbook. It may well have been written later than the play and have been influenced by some of the changes which Shakespeare made for dramatic purposes. The ballad was reprinted by Richard Johnson in his *Golden Garland of Princely Pleasures and Delicate Delights* of 1620, and it appears in some later ballad collections as well.

In an important article in *Studies in Philology* for 1949, Ralph M. Sargent has very closely compared the prose chapbook with Shakespeare's play, and he has come to the conclusion, now shared by most scholars, that in its putative sixteenth-century form the chapbook must have provided Shakespeare's major source. Although there are important differences, the prose story is very close to Shakespeare's play, and those elements in which Shakespeare's work differs from it seem to have been invented by him in order to shape the material in terms of a more consistent tragic design. Shakespeare's additions include almost all of the matter in the play's first act. There is no Alarbus in the prose story, and although Aaron does appear as a nameless Moorish captive, Shakespeare greatly develops this character from the source, where he is merely an agent of Tamora. Shakespeare fashioned Aaron in terms of the "Machiavellian" villain which had been made popular by the Lorenzo of Kyd's *Spanish Tragedy* and the Barabas of Marlowe's *Jew of Malta,* but he humanized him beyond anything in these earlier villains by such effective devices as showing him with his black child. The Moor of the source begs for mercy after his capture, but is tortured nevertheless, his body smeared with honey and left to be eaten by bees and wasps. Shakespeare's Aaron is endued with a savage pride which leaves him unrepentant and defiant in a way which looks forward to the Iago of *Othello.*

The source's account of the queen's feast upon the flesh and ground up bones of her sons probably suggested to Shakespeare two similar stories in Greek mythology which he interwove with his major source. The first and more important of these was that of the rape of Philomela which he must have read in Book VI of Ovid's *Metamorphoses,* and the other was that of the revenge of Atreus upon his brother Thyestes which is the subject of the *Thyestes* of Seneca. Both of these works were available to him in Latin and were, in fact, commonly read by Elizabethan schoolboys, but he may have read Ovid in the English translation of Arthur Golding printed in 1567 and *Thyestes* in that of Jasper Heywood printed in 1560.

In Ovid's account, Philomela goes to live with her sister, Progne (or Procne). Progne's husband, Tereus, King of Thrace, rapes Philomela, cuts off her tongue to insure her silence, and keeps her imprisoned, but she weaves the story of her fate into a tapestry which she sends to her sister. Progne liberates Philomela during a Bacchanalian revel and the two sisters plan revenge on Tereus. They kill Itys, Progne's son by Tereus, and serve him to his father on a dish. The women then flee from the palace with Tereus in pursuit. When he is about to kill them, they pray to the gods for help, and all three are turned into birds. Philomela becomes a nightingale and Progne a swallow; Tereus becomes a hawk so that he may continue to pursue them forever.

Seneca's *Thyestes* is concerned with one episode among the many atrocities which plague the house of Pelops. Its central figure is the deeply wronged avenger, Atreus, who, in a culminating act of vengeance against his brother, murders the two sons of

Thyestes in a ritual sacrifice, mixes their blood with wine, and causes Thyestes to feast in gluttony upon the flesh and blood of his own children. Both of these well known classical stories had already been used by the author of the prose account of Titus Andronicus, but Shakespeare gave them a prominence in his play beyond anything in his source. The strong Ovidian tone of Shakespeare's play has been noted by many critics. Lavinia is especially close to Ovid's Philomela, as she is to another victim of unnatural violation, the heroine of Shakespeare's own *Rape of Lucrece,* printed in 1594. Not only is *Titus Andronicus* full of direct references to this story, but the play contains many verbal parallels with Shakespeare's own poem, which may indicate Shakespeare's natural tendency to think of the two stories in similar terms, although it provides no evidence that the two works were written close to one another in time.

Of all the plays of Seneca, the *Thyestes* may have been the most influential in forming the vogue for tragedy of blood revenge which was so popular at the time Shakespeare began to write *Titus Andronicus,* and which is well exemplified by Thomas Kyd's *Spanish Tragedy,* which must have been one of Shakespeare's dramatic models, since the two plays reveal many common features. From Seneca came the theme of inevitable nemesis as punishment for unnatural crime, with blood calling for blood, each avenger exceeding in the horror of his own vengeance that of the crime from which he himself has suffered, and each avenger effecting his own destruction while he plots that of his adversary.

For some elements not in the prose source, Shakespeare seems to have turned to other plays of Seneca. For the rivalry between Saturninus and Bassianus, he probably took a suggestion from Seneca's *Thebans.* The sacrifice of Alarbus seems almost certainly to have been suggested by the *Troades,* where the children of defeated Trojans must be sacrificed to appease the spirit of Achilles. Scraps of Latin are quoted from the *Phaedra* and the *Hercules Furens.* In *Titus Andronicus,* as in no other of his plays, Shakespeare directs his audience to his own sources, as in having Lavinia call attention to the story of Philomela in Ovid. Throughout the play there is deliberate evocation in the poetic imagery of the specific characteristics of the Senecan underworld. For the political considerations which Shakespeare combined with his story in a way which looks forward to his Roman history plays, he seems to have been indebted to Thomas North's translation of *Plutarch's Lives* (1579), which was to serve as the source of his later Roman plays. Plutarch's life of Scipio seems especially to have furnished him with suggestions for the names of his characters.

TRAGIC DESIGN

Titus Andronicus has often been dismissed as a ridiculous play, full of horror and sensationalism for their own sakes, and at best no more than a young dramatist's halting attempt to imitate the crude Senecanism of his contemporaries, only partly redeemed by some passages of promising verse. The story with which Shakespeare worked, with its rape, mutilations, and final Thyestian banquet, allowed him ample scope to outdo the horrors that were fashionable in the plays of the time, and to shock and titillate an audience to the full. We must, however, recognize that upon this crude matter Shakespeare imposed a tragic design, a probing into the meaning of human disaster, which looks forward to what he was to achieve in his maturity. The surest evidence for Shakespeare's authorship may be in the seriousness with which he approached what might, in another's hand, have been either absurd melodrama or farce.

One of the keys to Shakespeare's transformation of his source is his use not only of Ovid's story of Philomela, but of the theme which runs throughout the *Metamorphoses,* that of the transformation of man into beast through excess of passion. Such a transformation Shakespeare reveals in his hero, who at the beginning of the play is a great and magnificent creature of commanding stature, political probity, and utter devotion to his country's good. The degeneration of such a man into a monster capable of committing the most unnatural of crimes is a truly tragic spectacle, and Shakespeare made some attempt to set this degeneration within a moral framework.

Titus, much like a later Coriolanus, reveals the source of his own destruction in the very nobility which makes him a dedicated servant of his country. He observes the principle of hereditary right which was dear to Elizabethans, refusing the crown when he might have it himself and giving his support to Saturninus, the elder son of the deceased emperor. His devotion to his family status and his duty as a lawful subject who must obey royal commands lead him to give his daughter to be his new emperor's consort, and in this he suffers from a conflict between public and personal obligation. His very devotion to country and family position creates in him a moral blindness that causes him to violate Lavinia's pledged troth to Bassianus, and arouses the fit of passion which causes him to slay his own son for opposition to his paternal will. Like King Lear, Titus suffers for his sins on a scale of great magnitude, and Shakespeare uses various means to win sympathy for him, revealing him with his grandchild, and emphasizing the general sorrow which accompanies his death. In the source Titus kills the emperor, but Shakespeare spares him the additional sin of regicide.

Shakespeare also tries to place the destruction of Titus within a larger framework in which evil too is destroyed, so that his audience, while lamenting the destruction of one heroic human soul, may leave the theatre with some sense of final reconciliation. Marcus points out the path which Titus might have taken, and Lucius brings about a regeneration in the state when the forces both of good and evil lie dead upon the stage and the world is ready for rebirth. In the portrait of the degeneration of a noble hero through traits which spring from those very qualities within him with which the audience may closely sympathize, and in the reconciliation which comes from the general destruction of evil in spite of his fall, we may find a design for tragedy which postulates the reality of evil, man's free moral choice in spite of it, and a sense of ultimate justice in the universe. That Shakespeare could at this early stage of his career infuse such a design into a story like that of Titus Andronicus reveals the beginning of a power and insight which will enable him one day to write such plays as *Othello, Lear,* and *Coriolanus.*

THE TRAGEDY OF
Titus Andronicus

[DRAMATIS PERSONÆ.

SATURNINUS, *son to the late Emperor of Rome, and afterwards declared Emperor.*

BASSIANUS, *brother to* SATURNINUS; *in love with* LAVINIA.

TITUS ANDRONICUS, *a Roman, General against the Goths.*

MARCUS ANDRONICUS, *Tribune of the People, brother to* TITUS.

LUCIUS,
QUINTUS,
MARTIUS,
MUTIUS, } *sons to* TITUS ANDRONICUS.

YOUNG LUCIUS, *a boy, son to* LUCIUS.

PUBLIUS, *son to* MARCUS ANDRONICUS.

SEMPRONIUS,
CAIUS,
VALENTINE, } *kinsmen to* TITUS ANDRONICUS.

ÆMILIUS, *a noble Roman.*

ALARBUS,
DEMETRIUS, } *sons to* TAMORA.
CHIRON,

AARON, *a Moor, beloved by* TAMORA.

A Captain.

A Messenger.

A Clown.

TAMORA, *Queen of the Goths.*

LAVINIA, *daughter to* TITUS ANDRONICUS.

A Nurse, and a black Child.

Romans and Goths, Senators, Tribunes, Officers, Soldiers, Attendants.

SCENE. — *Rome and the neighbourhood.*]

Act One

◇◇◇

SCENE I. [*Rome. Before the Capitol.*]

Flourish. Enter the Tribunes *and* Senators *aloft. And then
enter [below]* Saturninus *and his* Followers *at one door;
and* Bassianus *and his* Followers *at the other, with* Drums
and Trumpets.

SAT. Noble patricians, patrons of my right,
Defend the justice of my cause with arms.
And, countrymen, my loving followers,
Plead my successive title with your swords.
I am his first-born son that was the last   5
That ware the imperial diadem of Rome.
Then let my father's honours live in me,
Nor wrong mine age with this indignity.

BAS. Romans, friends, followers, favourers of my right,
If ever Bassianus, Cæsar's son,   10
Were gracious in the eyes of royal Rome,
Keep then this passage to the Capitol;
And suffer not dishonour to approach
The imperial seat, to virtue consecrate,
To justice, continence, and nobility;   15

I.I. 4 *successive title* right of succession to the throne.   5 *his . . . last* the eldest
son of him who was the last.   6 *ware* wore. *diadem* crown.   8 *mine age* my
rights as the eldest son. *this indignity* i.e. being denied the throne in favour of
a younger brother.   11 *gracious* acceptable.   12 *Keep* defend.   13 *suffer not* do
not permit.   15 *continence* self-restraint (chiefly in the exercise of power).

But let desert in pure election shine;
And, Romans, fight for freedom in your choice.

Enter Marcus Andronicus, aloft, with
the crown.

MARC. Princes that strive by factions and by friends
Ambitiously for rule and empery,
Know that the people of Rome, for whom we stand   20
A special party, have by common voice
In election for the Roman empery
Chosen Andronicus, surnamed Pius
For many good and great deserts to Rome.
A nobler man, a braver warrior,   25
Lives not this day within the city walls.
He by the Senate is accited home
From weary wars against the barbarous Goths,
That with his sons (a terror to our foes)
Hath yok'd a nation strong, train'd up in arms.   30
Ten years are spent since first he undertook
This cause of Rome, and chastised with arms
Our enemies' pride. Five times he hath return'd
Bleeding to Rome, bearing his valiant sons
In coffins from the field;   35
And now at last, laden with honour's spoils,
Returns the good Andronicus to Rome,
Renowned Titus, flourishing in arms.
Let us entreat by honour of his name
Whom (worthily) you would have now succeed,   40
And in the Capitol and Senate's right,
Whom you pretend to honour and adore,
That you withdraw you and abate your strength,
Dismiss your followers, and, as suitors should,

16 *let desert . . . shine* let merit prevail in a true election (on the basis of worth
rather than the claim of primogeniture).   18 *factions* parties.   19 *empery* the
right to be emperor.   24 *deserts* meritorious deeds.   27 *accited* summoned.   30
yok'd subjugated, placed under the yoke of Rome.   31 *are spent* have passed.
35 *from the field* At this point Q¹ inserts the following lines: "and at this day,/To
the monument of that Andronicy/Done sacrifice of expiation,/And slaine the

	Plead your deserts in peace and humbleness.	45
SAT.	How fair the Tribune speaks to calm my thoughts!	
BAS.	Marcus Andronicus, so I do affy	
	In thy uprightness and integrity,	
	And so I love and honour thee and thine,	
	Thy noble brother Titus and his sons,	50
	And her to whom my thoughts are humbled all,	
	Gracious Lavinia, Rome's rich ornament,	
	That I will here dismiss my loving friends	
	And to my fortune's and the people's favour	
	Commit my cause in balance to be weigh'd.	55

Exeunt Soldiers [*and other* Followers *of* Bassianus].

SAT.	Friends that have been thus forward in my right,	
	I thank you all and here dismiss you all,	
	And to the love and favour of my country	
	Commit myself, my person, and the cause.	

[*Exeunt the* Followers *of* Saturinus.]

	Rome, be as just and gracious unto me	60
	As I am confident and kind to thee.	
	Open the gates and let me in.	
BAS.	Tribunes, and me, a poor competitor.	

Flourish. They go up into the Senate House.

Enter a Captain.

CAPT.	Romans, make way. The good Andronicus,	
	Patron of virtue, Rome's best champion,	65

Noblest prisoner of the Gothes." They were omitted in Q², Q³, and F¹, and rightly so, since they are contradicted by the rest of the scene. They probably were intended for deletion in Shakespeare's foul papers and printed accidentally in Q¹. The error was caught by the Q² editor.   42 *pretend* profess, claim.   43 *abate* lessen.   46 *fair* civilly.   47 *affy* trust.   61 *confident* trusting. *kind* full of natural feeling.   63 *competitor* rival.   65 *Patron* pattern, model.

Successful in the battles that he fights,
With honour and with fortune is return'd
From where he circumscribed with his sword
And brought to yoke the enemies of Rome.

> *Sound drums and trumpets; and then
> enter two of* Titus' *sons,* [Martius *and*
> Mutius;] *and then two men bearing a
> coffin covered with black; then* [Lu-
> cius *and* Quintus,] *two other sons;
> then* Titus Andronicus; *and then*
> Tamora, *the Queen of Goths, and her
> two sons,* Chiron *and* Demetrius, *with*
> Aaron *the Moor and others, as many
> as can be,* [*including* Tamora's *son*
> Alarbus *and other Goths, prisoners*].
> *Then set down the coffin, and* Titus
> *speaks.*

TIT.   Hail, Rome, victorious in thy mourning weeds!   70
       Lo, as the bark that hath discharg'd his fraught
       Returns with precious lading to the bay
       From whence at first she weigh'd her anchorage,
       Cometh Andronicus, bound with laurel boughs,
       To resalute his country with his tears,   75
       Tears of true joy for his return to Rome.
       Thou great defender of this Capitol,
       Stand gracious to the rites that we intend!
       Romans, of five-and-twenty valiant sons,
       Half of the number that King Priam had,   80
       Behold the poor remains, alive and dead!
       These that survive let Rome reward with love;
       These that I bring unto their latest home,

---

68 *circumscribed* encompassed, brought within the bounds of rule.   70 *weeds* garments.   71 *bark* ship.   *his fraught* its cargo (Q¹; F², K: "her fraught").   72 *lading*
cargo.   73 *anchorage* anchors.   74 *laurel boughs* the traditional symbol of victory.
77 *Thou great defender* Jupiter.   80 *Priam* King of Troy.   83 *latest home* final
resting place.   86 *unkind* unnatural.   *careless of* without proper regard for.   88
To hover . . . Styx The souls of unburied men were not permitted to cross the
river Styx, and thus could not enter Hades.   89 *bretheren* This spelling is retained

With burial amongst their ancestors.
Here Goths have given me leave to sheathe my sword.   85
Titus unkind, and careless of thine own,
Why suffer'st thou thy sons, unburied yet,
To hover on the dreadful shore of Styx?
Make way to lay them by their bretheren.

They open the tomb.

There greet in silence, as the dead are wont,   90
And sleep in peace, slain in your country's wars.
O sacred receptacle of my joys,
Sweet cell of virtue and nobility,
How many sons hast thou of mine in store
That thou wilt never render to me more!   95

LUC.   Give us the proudest prisoner of the Goths,
That we may hew his limbs and on a pile
Ad manes fratrum sacrifice his flesh
Before this earthy prison of their bones,
That so the shadows be not unappeas'd,   100
Nor we disturb'd with prodigies on earth.

TIT.   I give him you — the noblest that survives,
The eldest son of this distressed queen.

TAM.   Stay, Roman brethren! Gracious conqueror,
Victorious Titus, rue the tears I shed,   105
A mother's tears in passion for her son;
And if thy sons were ever dear to thee,
O, think my son to be as dear to me!
Sufficeth not that we are brought to Rome
To beautify thy triumphs, and return   110
Captive to thee and to thy Roman yoke;

---

throughout when the metre requires it.   92 *receptacle* sepulchre, tomb.   95
render give back.   96 *proudest* most noble.   97 *pile* funeral pyre.   98 *Ad manes
fratrum* to the spirits of our brothers.   *manes* F³; Q¹: "manus."   100 *shadows*
ghosts.   101 *with prodigies* by unnatural phenomena (such as might occur if the
spirits remained angry). Such events were signs of disaster.   110 *beautify thy
triumphs* adorn your triumphal celebration.

But must my sons be slaughtered in the streets
For valiant doings in their country's cause?
O, if to fight for king and commonweal
Were piety in thine, it is in these!   115
Andronicus, stain not thy tomb with blood.
Wilt thou draw near the nature of the gods?
Draw near them then in being merciful.
Sweet mercy is nobility's true badge.
Thrice-noble Titus, spare my first-born son!   120

TIT.   Patient yourself, madam, and pardon me.
These are their brethren, whom your Goths beheld
Alive and dead; and for their brethren slain
Religiously they ask a sacrifice.
To this your son is mark'd, and die he must   125
T' appease their groaning shadows that are gone.

LUC.   Away with him, and make a fire straight,
And with our swords, upon a pile of wood,
Let's hew his limbs till they be clean consum'd.

                  Exeunt Titus' sons *with* Alarbus.

TAM.   O cruel irreligious piety!   130

CHI.   Was never Scythia half so barbarous.

DEM.   Oppose not Scythia to ambitious Rome.
Alarbus goes to rest, and we survive
To tremble under Titus' threat'ning look.
Then, madam, stand resolv'd; but hope withal,   135
The selfsame gods that arm'd the Queen of Troy
With opportunity of sharp revenge
Upon the Thracian tyrant in his tent
May favour Tamora, the Queen of Goths
(When Goths were Goths, and Tamora was queen),   140

---

116 *tomb* family vault.   121 *Patient yourself* compose yourself.   125 *mark'd* destined.   126 *their groaning . . . gone* the lamenting spirits of those who are gone.   131 *Scythia* a region in southern Russia proverbial for the savagery of its inhabitants.   132 *Oppose* compare.   135 *stand* resolv'd be resolute. *withal* as well.   136 *Queen of Troy* Hecuba, who, after the fall of Troy, became the

To quit the bloody wrongs upon her foes.

> *Enter* [Lucius, Quintus, Martius, *and*
> Mutius,] *the sons of* Andronicus,
> *again,* [*with their swords bloody*].

LUC.   See, lord and father, how we have perform'd
       Our Roman rites. Alarbus' limbs are lopp'd
       And entrails feed the sacrificing fire,
       Whose smoke like incense doth perfume the sky.   145
       Remaineth naught but to inter our brethren
       And with loud 'larums welcome them to Rome.

TIT.   Let it be so, and let Andronicus
       Make this his latest farewell to their souls.

> *Sound trumpets, and lay the coffin in
> the tomb.*

       In peace and honour rest you here, my sons;   150
       Rome's readiest champions, repose you here in rest,
       Secure from worldly chances and mishaps!
       Here lurks no treason, here no envy swells,
       Here grow no damned drugs, here are no storms,
       No noise, but silence and eternal sleep.   155
       In peace and honour rest you here, my sons!

> *Enter* Lavinia.

LAV.   In peace and honour live Lord Titus long!
       My noble lord and father, live in fame!
       Lo, at this tomb my tributary tears
       I render for my brethren's obsequies;   160
       And at thy feet I kneel with tears of joy
       Shed on this earth for thy return to Rome.
       O, bless me here with thy victorious hand,
       Whose fortunes Rome's best citizens applaud!

---

slave of Polynestor, whose two sons she murdered in revenge for the murder of
her own son, Polydorus.   137 *sharp* bitter.   138 *Thracian tyrant* Polynestor.   141
quit requite, revenge.   147 *'larums* alarums, sounds of the trumpet.   149 *latest*
final.   153 *envy* malice.   154 *drugs* poison producing plants.   159 *tributary
tears* tears offered in tribute.   160 *obsequies* funeral rites.

TIT.   Kind Rome, that hast thus lovingly reserv'd   165
           The cordial of mine age to glad my heart!
           Lavinia, live; outlive thy father's days,
           And fame's eternal date, for virtue's praise!

                       [*Enter, below,* Marcus Andronicus *and*
                       Tribunes. *Enter* Saturninus *and* Bas-
                       sianus, *attended.*]

MARC.   Long live Lord Titus, my beloved brother,
           Gracious triumpher in the eyes of Rome!   170

TIT.   Thanks, gentle Tribune, noble brother Marcus.

MARC.   And welcome, nephews, from successful wars,
           You that survive, and you that sleep in fame!
           Fair lords, your fortunes are alike in all
           That in your country's service drew your swords;   175
           But safer triumph is this funeral pomp
           That hath aspir'd to Solon's happiness
           And triumphs over chance in honour's bed.
           Titus Andronicus, the people of Rome,
           Whose friend in justice thou hast ever been,   180
           Send thee by me, their Tribune and their trust,
           This palliament of white and spotless hue;
           And name thee in election for the empire
           With these our late-deceased Emperor's sons.
           Be candidatus then, and put it on,   185
           And help to set a head on headless Rome.

TIT.   A better head her glorious body fits
           Than his that shakes for age and feebleness.
           What should I don this robe, and trouble you?
           Be chosen with proclamations to-day,   190

---

166 *cordial* comfort; literally, that which warms the heart.   *glad* make glad.   168
fame's eternal date fame which lasts forever.   177 *aspir'd* risen. *Solon's happiness*
When Croesus boasted to Solon of his happiness, Solon reportedly replied that
no man could be called truly happy until he was dead. The story is in Herodotus.
Thus those who have died in battle are more happy than those who live, for they
have escaped the possibility of future sorrow.   181 *their trust* one whom they
trust.   182 *palliament* ceremonial white robe.   183 *in election* as a candidate.

	To-morrow yield up rule, resign my life,
	And set abroad new business for you all?
	Rome, I have been thy soldier forty years,
	And led my country's strength successfully,
	And buried one-and-twenty valiant sons,	195
	Knighted in field, slain manfully in arms
	In right and service of their noble country.
	Give me a staff of honour for mine age,
	But not a sceptre to control the world.
	Upright he held it, lords, that held it last.	200

MARC.   Titus, thou shalt obtain and ask the empery.

SAT.   Proud and ambitious Tribune, canst thou tell?

TIT.   Patience, Prince Saturnine.

SAT.   Romans, do me right!
Patricians, draw your swords, and sheathe them not
Till Saturninus be Rome's Emperor.   205
Andronicus, would thou were shipp'd to hell
Rather than rob me of the people's hearts!

LUC.   Proud Saturnine, interrupter of the good
That noble-minded Titus means to thee!

TIT.   Content thee, prince. I will restore to thee   210
The people's hearts, and wean them from themselves.

BAS.   Andronicus, I do not flatter thee,
But honour thee, and will do till I die.
My faction if thou strengthen with thy friends,
I will most thankful be; and thanks to men   215
Of noble minds is honourable meed.

TIT.   People of Rome, and People's Tribunes here,

---

the empire the title of emperor.   185 *candidatus* a candidate. The word is Latin
for "white-robed."   188 *for* because of.   189 *What* why.   192 *set abroad* set on
foot, put in motion (Q¹; Q³, к: "set abroach").   197 *In right . . . country* in de-
fence of the just cause of and in service to their noble country.   201 *obtain and
ask* obtain if you ask.   202 *canst thou tell* how can you be certain?   211 *wean
. . . themselves* i.e. cause them to alter their opinions (and choose you as emperor).
214 *faction* party of supporters.   216 *meed* reward.

I ask your voices and your suffrages.
Will ye bestow them friendly on Andronicus?

TRIBUNES. To gratify the good Andronicus,   220
    And gratulate his safe return to Rome,
    The people will accept whom he admits.

TIT.   Tribunes, I thank you; and this suit I make,
    That you create our Emperor's eldest son,
    Lord Saturnine; whose virtues will, I hope,   225
    Reflect on Rome as Titan's rays on earth
    And ripen justice in this commonweal.
    Then, if you will elect by my advice,
    Crown him and say "Long live our Emperor!"

MARC.   With voices and applause of every sort,   230
    Patricians and plebeians, we create
    Lord Saturninus Rome's great Emperor
    And say "Long live our Emperor Saturnine!"

                A long flourish till they come down.

SAT.   Titus Andronicus, for thy favours done
    To us in our election this day   235
    I give thee thanks in part of thy deserts,
    And will with deeds requite thy gentleness;
    And for an onset, Titus, to advance
    Thy name and honourable family,
    Lavinia will I make my emperess,   240
    Rome's royal mistress, mistress of my heart,
    And in the sacred Pantheon her espouse.
    Tell me, Andronicus, doth this motion please thee?

TIT.   It doth, my worthy lord, and in this match
    I hold me highly honoured of your Grace;   245

---

218 *voices* votes.   219 *friendly* as friends.   221 *gratulate* rejoice at, commemorate.
222 *whom he admits* whomever he chooses.   226 *Reflect on* (a) shine upon (b)
bring credit to.   *Titan's* the sun god's.   227 *ripen justice* cause justice to grow
and mature (as the sun does with crops).   236 *in part of* in partial reward for.
237 *requite* repay.   *gentleness* true nobility.   238 *onset* beginning.   *advance* raise
in rank.   242 *Pantheon* the Roman temple dedicated to all of the gods (F²; QQ,
F¹: "Pathan").   243 *motion* offer, proposal.   245 *hold me* consider myself.   250

And here in sight of Rome, to Saturnine,
King and commander of our commonweal,
The wide world's Emperor, do I consecrate
My sword, my chariot, and my prisoners,
Presents well worthy Rome's imperious lord.   250
Receive them then, the tribute that I owe,
Mine honour's ensigns humbled at thy feet.

SAT. Thanks, noble Titus, father of my life.
How proud I am of thee and of thy gifts
Rome shall record; and when I do forget   255
The least of these unspeakable deserts,
Romans, forget your fealty to me.

TIT. [*to* Tamora] Now, madam, are you prisoner to an em-
peror,
To him that, for your honour and your state,
Will use you nobly and your followers.   260

SAT. [*aside*] A goodly lady, trust me; of the hue
That I would choose, were I to choose anew. —
Clear up, fair Queen, that cloudy countenance.
Though chance of war hath wrought this change of cheer,
Thou com'st not to be made a scorn in Rome.   265
Princely shall be thy usage every way.
Rest on my word, and let not discontent
Daunt all your hopes. Madam, he comforts you
Can make you greater than the Queen of Goths.
Lavinia, you are not displeas'd with this?   270

LAV. Not I, my lord, sith true nobility
Warrants these words in princely courtesy.

SAT. Thanks, sweet Lavinia. Romans, let us go.
Ransomless here we set our prisoners free.

---

imperious imperial.   252 *Mine . . . humbled* the symbols of the honours I have
won placed humbly.   256 *unspeakable deserts* merits too great to be described.
257 *fealty* allegiance.   259 *for* because of. *state* high position.   261 *hue* complexion.   263 *cloudy* troubled, sad.   264 *chance* Q²; Q¹: "change." *cheer* countenance.   265 *scorn* object of scorn.   266 *usage* treatment.   267 *Rest* depend.
268 *he* he who.   271 *sith* since.   272 *Warrants* justifies.

Proclaim our honours, lords, with trump and drum.   275

> [*Flourish.*]

BAS. Lord Titus, by your leave, this maid is mine.

> [*Seizes* Lavinia.]

TIT. How, sir? Are you in earnest then, my lord?

BAS. Ay, noble Titus, and resolv'd withal
To do myself this reason and this right.

MARC. *Suum cuique* is our Roman justice.   280
This prince in justice seizeth but his own.

LUC. And that he will and shall, if Lucius live.

TIT. Traitors, avaunt! Where is the Emperor's guard?
Treason, my lord! Lavinia is surpris'd!

SAT. Surpris'd? By whom?

BAS.   By him that justly may   285
Bear his betroth'd from all the world away.

> [*Exeunt* Bassianus *and* Marcus *with*
> Lavinia.]

MUTIUS. Brothers, help to convey her hence away,
And with my sword I'll keep this door safe.

> [*Exeunt* Lucius, Quintus, *and* Mar-
> tius.]

TIT. Follow, my lord, and I'll soon bring her back.

MUTIUS. My lord, you pass not here.

TIT.   What, villain boy?   290
Bar'st me my way in Rome?

MUTIUS.   Help, Lucius, help!

> [Titus] *kills him.*

---

275 *trump* trumpet.   278 *resolv'd withal* determined also.   279 *reason* justice.
280 *Suum cuique* to each his own. *cuique* F²; Q¹: "cuiqum."   283 *avaunt* be gone.
284 *surpris'd* captured.   301 *by leisure* not quickly or readily.   304 *none in Rome*
Q¹; F², K: "there none els in Rome." F²'s attempt to improve upon Shakespeare's

[*During the fray, exeunt* Saturninus, Tamora, Demetrius, Chiron, *and* Aaron.]

[*Enter* Lucius.]

LUC.   My lord, you are unjust, and more than so!
In wrongful quarrel you have slain your son.

TIT.   Nor thou nor he are any sons of mine;
My sons would never so dishonour me.   295

Enter aloft the Emperor *with* Tamora *and her two* Sons, *and* Aaron *the* Moor.

Traitor, restore Lavinia to the Emperor.

LUC.   Dead, if you will; but not to be his wife,
That is another's lawful promis'd love.   [*Exit.*]

SAT.   No, Titus, no. The Emperor needs her not —
Nor her, nor thee, nor any of thy stock.   300
I'll trust by leisure him that mocks me once;
Thee never, nor thy traitorous haughty sons,
Confederates all thus to dishonour me.
Was none in Rome to make a stale
But Saturnine? Full well, Andronicus,   305
Agree these deeds with that proud brag of thine
That saidst I begg'd the empire at thy hands.

TIT.   O monstrous! What reproachful words are these?

SAT.   But go thy ways! Go give that changing piece
To him that flourish'd for her with his sword!   310
A valiant son-in-law thou shalt enjoy;
One fit to bandy with thy lawless sons,
To ruffle in the commonwealth of Rome.

TIT.   These words are razors to my wounded heart.

---

metre can have no textual authority. *stale* laughingstock.   **309** *changing piece* fickle slut.   **310** *flourish'd . . . sword* brandished his sword in order to win her. **312** *bandy* brawl.   **313** *ruffle* swagger.

SAT.   And therefore, lovely Tamora, Queen of Goths,   315
That, like the stately Phœbe 'mongst her nymphs,
Dost overshine the gallant'st dames of Rome,
If thou be pleas'd with this my sudden choice,
Behold, I choose thee, Tamora, for my bride
And will create thee Emperess of Rome.   320
Speak, Queen of Goths, dost thou applaud my choice?
And here I swear by all the Roman gods —
Sith priest and holy water are so near,
And tapers burn so bright, and everything
In readiness for Hymenæus stand —   325
I will not resalute the streets of Rome
Or climb my palace till from forth this place
I lead espous'd my bride along with me.

TAM.   And here in sight of heaven to Rome I swear,
If Saturnine advance the Queen of Goths,   330
She will a handmaid be to his desires,
A loving nurse, a mother to his youth.

SAT.   Ascend, fair Queen, Pantheon. Lords, accompany
Your noble Emperor and his lovely bride,
Sent by the heavens for Prince Saturnine,   335
Whose wisdom hath her fortune conquered.
There shall we consummate our spousal rites.

                                    Exeunt [*all but* Titus].

TIT.   I am not bid to wait upon this bride.
Titus, when wert thou wont to walk alone,
Dishonoured thus and challenged of wrongs?   340

                        Enter Marcus *and* Titus' Sons — [Lu-
                        cius, Quintus, *and* Martius].

MARC.   O Titus, see! O, see what thou hast done!

---

316 *Phœbe* Diana, goddess of the moon and of chastity (F²; QQ, F¹: "Thebe").   317
overshine shine brighter than.   321 *applaud* approve.   323 *Sith* since.   324
tapers candles, traditionally used in Roman wedding ceremonies.   325 *Hymenæus*
Hymen, god of marriage.   326 *resalute* greet again.   330 *advance* raise in status.
331 *handmaid* servant.   336 *Whose . . . conquered* who by her wisdom (in ac-
cepting Saturnine) has overcome her bad fortune (in being a captive).   337 *spousal*

        In a bad quarrel slain a virtuous son.

TIT.   No, foolish Tribune, no! no son of mine —
        Nor thou, nor these, confederates in the deed
        That hath dishonoured all our family;   345
        Unworthy brother, and unworthy sons!

LUC.   But let us give him burial as becomes;
        Give Mutius burial with our bretheren.

TIT.   Traitors, away! He rests not in this tomb!
        This monument five hundreth years hath stood,   350
        Which I have sumptuously reëdified.
        Here none but soldiers and Rome's servitors
        Repose in fame; none basely slain in brawls.
        Bury him where you can, he comes not here.

MARC.   My lord, this is impiety in you.   355
        My nephew Mutius' deeds do plead for him;
        He must be buried with his bretheren.

               Titus' *two* sons *speak*.

[QUINT., MART.] And shall, or him we will accompany.

TIT.   "And shall"? What villain was it spake that word?

               Titus' son *speaks*.

[QUINT.] He that would vouch it in any place but here.   360

TIT.   What, would you bury him in my despite?

MARC.   No, noble Titus, but entreat of thee
        To pardon Mutius and to bury him.

TIT.   Marcus, even thou hast stroke upon my crest,
        And with these boys mine honour thou hast wounded.   365
        My foes I do repute you every one;

---

marriage. 338 *bid* asked. 339 *wont* accustomed. 340 *challenged* accused. 342
bad quarrel wrong cause. 347 *becomes* is fitting. 350 *hundreth* A common
Elizabethan form. 351 *reëdified* rebuilt. 352 *servitors* armed defenders. 360
vouch maintain. 361 *in my despite* in spite of my opposition. 364 *stroke*
struck. *crest* the coronet above a coat of arms, symbolic of a man's honour. 366
repute consider.

SO trouble me no more, but get you gone.

3. SON [MART.] He is not with himself. Let us withdraw.

2. SON [QUINT.] Not I, till Mutius' bones be buried.

The Brother *and the* Sons *kneel.*

MARC.   Brother, for in that name doth nature plead —   370

2. SON [QUINT.] Father, and in that name doth nature speak —

TIT.   Speak thou no more, if all the rest will speed.

MARC.   Renowmed Titus, more than half my soul —

LUC.   Dear father, soul and substance of us all —

MARC.   Suffer thy brother Marcus to inter   375
         His noble nephew here in virtue's nest,
         That died in honour and Lavinia's cause.
         Thou art a Roman; be not barbarous.
         The Greeks upon advice did bury Ajax,
         That slew himself; and wise Laertes' son   380
         Did graciously plead for his funerals.
         Let not young Mutius then, that was thy joy,
         Be barr'd his entrance here.

TIT.   Rise, Marcus, rise.

[They rise.]

         The dismall'st day is this that e'er I saw,
         To be dishonoured by my sons in Rome.   385
         Well, bury him, and bury me the next.

They put him in the tomb.

LUC.   There lie thy bones, sweet Mutius, with thy friends,
         Till we with trophies do adorn thy tomb!

---

368 *not with himself* out of his mind.   372 *Speak thou . . . speed* the less you
speak the better it will be for the others. *speed* fare.   373 *Renowmed* renowned
(a common variant form).   379–81 *The Greeks . . . his funerals* Because the
arms of Achilles were given to Ulysses rather than Ajax, Ajax went mad and
killed himself. The Greeks, upon the advice of Ulysses (wise Laertes' son) gave him
honourable burial. The story was available to Shakespeare in various places. *upon*

They all kneel and say:

No man shed tears for noble Mutius!
He lives in fame that died in virtue's cause.   390

> [*They rise, and*] *all but* Marcus *and*
> Titus [*stand aside*].

MARC. My lord — to step out of these dreary dumps —
How comes it that the subtile Queen of Goths
Is of a sudden thus advanc'd in Rome?

TIT. I know not, Marcus; but I know it is —
Whether by device or no, the heavens can tell.   395
Is she not then beholding to the man
That brought her for this high good turn so far?
Yes, and will nobly him remunerate.

> *Flourish. Enter the* Emperor, Tamora
> *and her two* Sons, *with the* Moor, *at*
> *one door. Enter at the other door* Bas-
> sianus *and* Lavinia, *with others.*

SAT. So, Bassianus, you have play'd your prize.
God give you joy, sir, of your gallant bride!   400

BAS. And you of yours, my lord! I say no more
Nor wish no less, and so I take my leave.

SAT. Traitor, if Rome have law or we have power,
Thou and thy faction shall repent this rape.

BAS. Rape call you it, my lord, to seize my own,   405
My true betrothed love, and now my wife?
But let the laws of Rome determine all;
Meanwhile am I possess'd of that is mine.

SAT. 'Tis good, sir. You are very short with us;

---

advice after due consideration. *graciously* so as to win acceptance. 388 *trophies*
memorial tokens. 391 *dumps* melancholy. 392 *subtile* subtle, crafty. 395
device deliberate scheming. 396 *beholding* indebted. 398 *Yes . . . remunerate*
F¹; not in QQ. Some editors give the line to Marcus and may well be correct. 399
play'd your prize won your match. The expression is from fencing. 408 *that*
what. 409 *short* curt.

But if we live, we'll be as sharp with you.   410

BAS.   My lord, what I have done, as best I may
Answer I must, and shall do with my life.
Only thus much I give your Grace to know:
By all the duties that I owe to Rome,
This noble gentleman, Lord Titus here,   415
Is in opinion and in honour wrong'd,
That, in the rescue of Lavinia,
With his own hand did slay his youngest son,
In zeal to you, and highly mov'd to wrath
To be controll'd in that he frankly gave.   420
Receive him then to favour, Saturnine,
That hath express'd himself in all his deeds
A father and a friend to thee and Rome.

TIT.   Prince Bassianus, leave to plead my deeds.
'Tis thou, and those, that have dishonoured me.   425
Rome and the righteous heavens be my judge
How I have lov'd and honoured Saturnine!

TAM.   My worthy lord, if ever Tamora
Were gracious in those princely eyes of thine,
Then hear me speak indifferently for all;   430
And at my suit, sweet, pardon what is past.

SAT.   What, madam? be dishonoured openly
And basely put it up without revenge?

TAM.   Not so, my lord. The gods of Rome forfend
I should be author to dishonour you!   435
But on mine honour dare I undertake
For good Lord Titus' innocence in all;
Whose fury not dissembled speaks his griefs.
Then at my suit look graciously on him:
Lose not so noble a friend on vain suppose,   440

---

412 *Answer* account for.   416 *opinion* reputation.   420 *controll'd* thwarted,
rebuked. *that* what. *frankly* freely.   422 *express'd* revealed.   424 *leave to plead*
stop pleading.   429 *gracious* well regarded.   430 *indifferently for all* impartially
in so far as everyone is concerned.   433 *put it up* accept it.   434 *forfend* forbid.
435 *I should . . . you* that I should be responsible for any action that might dishonour you.   436 *undertake* vouch.   438 *speaks* gives evidence of.   439 *graciously*

  Nor with sour looks afflict his gentle heart.
  [*Aside to* Sat.] My lord, be rul'd by me, be won at last;
  Dissemble all your griefs and discontents.
  You are but newly planted in your throne;
  Lest, then, the people, and patricians too,   445
  Upon a just survey take Titus' part,
  And so supplant you for ingratitude,
  Which Rome reputes to be a heinous sin,
  Yield at entreats; and then let me alone:
  I'll find a day to massacre them all   450
  And rase their faction and their family,
  The cruel father and his traitorous sons,
  To whom I sued for my dear son's life;
  And make them know what 'tis to let a queen
  Kneel in the streets and beg for grace in vain. — 455
  Come, come, sweet Emperor. — Come, Andronicus. —
  Take up this good old man, and cheer the heart
  That dies in tempest of thy angry frown.

SAT. Rise, Titus, rise; my empress hath prevail'd.

TIT. I thank your Majesty, and her, my lord.   460
  These words, these looks, infuse new life in me.

TAM. Titus, I am incorporate in Rome,
  A Roman now adopted happily,
  And must advise the Emperor for his good.
  This day all quarrels die, Andronicus.   465
  And let it be mine honour, good my lord,
  That I have reconcil'd your friends and you.
  For you, Prince Bassianus, I have pass'd
  My word and promise to the Emperor
  That you will be more mild and tractable. 470
  And fear not, lords — and you, Lavinia.

---

with favour. 440 *on vain suppose* because of idle suspicion. 441 *gentle* noble.
443 *griefs* grievances. 446 *Upon . . . survey* upon careful study of the situation.
447 *supplant* remove. 448 *reputes* considers. 449 *at entreats* to entreaties. *let
me alone* leave matters to me. 451 *rase* root out, destroy. 457 *Take up* raise
to his feet. 462 *am incorporate in* have become a part of. 463 *happily* for-
tunately. 468 *pass'd* given.

By my advice, all humbled on your knees
You shall ask pardon of his Majesty.

[*Marcus, Lavinia, and the* Sons *of
Titus kneel.*]

SON [LUC.] We do, and vow to heaven and to his Highness
That what we did was mildly as we might,   475
Tend'ring our sister's honour and our own.

MARC.   That on mine honour here do I protest.

SAT.   Away, and talk not. Trouble us no more.

TAM.   Nay, nay, sweet Emperor, we must all be friends.
The Tribune and his nephews kneel for grace.   480
I will not be denied! Sweet heart, look back.

SAT.   Marcus, for thy sake and thy brother's here,
And at my lovely Tamora's entreats,
I do remit these young men's heinous faults. Stand up!

[*They rise.*]

Lavinia, though you left me like a churl,   485
I found a friend; and sure as death I swore
I would not part a bachelor from the priest.
Come, if the Emperor's court can feast two brides,
You are my guest, Lavinia, and your friends.
This day shall be a love-day, Tamora.   490

TIT.   To-morrow, an it please your Majesty
To hunt the panther and the hart with me,
With horn and hound we'll give your Grace bonjour.

SAT.   Be it so, Titus, and gramercy too.

Exeunt. Sound trumpets.

474-6 *We do . . . our own* F¹; Q¹ adds these lines to Tamora's previous speech.
475 *mildly as we might* done as mildly as was possible to us.   476 *Tend'ring*
having consideration for.   477 *protest* affirm.   483 *entreats* entreaties.   484
remit pardon. *faults* offences.   485 *like a churl* rudely, like a base peasant.   486
friend sweetheart.   487 *part . . . priest* depart from the priest still a bachelor.
490 *love-day* (a) day traditionally set aside for the settling of disputes (b) day
devoted to love.   493 *bonjour* good day.   494 *gramercy* thanks.

Act Two

[SCENE 1. *Rome. Before the Palace.*]

Enter Aaron *alone.*

AAR.　Now climbeth Tamora Olympus' top,
　　　Safe out of Fortune's shot, and sits aloft,
　　　Secure of thunder's crack or lightning flash,
　　　Advanc'd above pale envy's threat'ning reach.
　　　As when the golden sun salutes the morn　　　　　5
　　　And, having gilt the ocean with his beams,
　　　Gallops the zodiac in his glistering coach
　　　And overlooks the highest-peering hills,
　　　So Tamora.
　　　Upon her wit doth earthly honour wait,　　　　　10
　　　And virtue stoops and trembles at her frown.
　　　Then, Aaron, arm thy heart and fit thy thoughts
　　　To mount aloft with thy imperial mistress,
　　　And mount her pitch whom thou in triumph long
　　　Hast prisoner held, fett'red in amorous chains,　　15
　　　And faster bound to Aaron's charming eyes
　　　Than is Prometheus tied to Caucasus.

II.I. 1 *Olympus' top* the home of the Greeks gods.　3 *of* from.　4 *Advanc'd*
raised.　*envy* malice.　5 *salutes* greets.　7 *zodiac* the path of the sun.　8 *overlooks* looks down upon.　10 *Upon . . . wait* earthly honours depend upon her
wisdom, just as a servant is controlled by his master.　14 *mount her pitch* ascend
to her height. The "pitch" is literally the highest point reached by a falcon in
its flight.　16 *faster* more securely.　*charming* bewitching, spell casting.　17
Prometheus the Titan who was bound by Zeus to a rock in the Caucasus as punishment for his stealing fire from the gods and giving it to man.

Away with slavish weeds and servile thoughts!
I will be bright and shine in pearl and gold,
To wait upon this new-made emperess.   20
To wait, said I? To wanton with this queen,
This goddess, this Semiramis, this nymph,
This siren that will charm Rome's Saturnine
And see his shipwrack and his commonweal's.
Holloa! what storm is this?   25

Enter Chiron *and* Demetrius, *braving.*

DEM.   Chiron, thy years wants wit, thy wits wants edge
And manners, to intrude where I am grac'd
And may, for aught thou knowest, affected be.

CHI.   Demetrius, thou dost overween in all;
And so in this, to bear me down with braves.   30
'Tis not the difference of a year or two
Makes me less gracious, or thee more fortunate.
I am as able and as fit as thou
To serve, and to deserve my mistress' grace;
And that my sword upon thee shall approve,   35
And plead my passions for Lavinia's love.

AAR.   [*aside*] Clubs, clubs! These lovers will not keep the peace.

DEM.   Why, boy, although our mother (unadvis'd)
Gave you a dancing rapier by your side,
Are you so desperate grown to threat your friends?   40
Go to! Have your lath glued within your sheath
Till you know better how to handle it.

CHI.   Meanwhile, sir, with the little skill I have,

---

18 *weeds* garments. *servile* lowly, obsequious.   20 *wait upon* attend, serve.   21
wanton sport amorously.   22 *Semiramis* the legendary wife of Ninus, the founder
of the Assyrian Empire, known for her beauty, ambition, and lust.   25 *s.d. braving*
talking loudly and arrogantly.   26 *years wants* A singular verb with a collective
subject is common Elizabethan diction.   *thy wits* Q¹; Q², κ: "thy wit."   27 *grac'd*
favoured.   28 *affected* loved.   29 *overween* behave with arrogance, presume
more than you should.   30 *bear me down* overwhelm me, get the best of me.
braves blustering threats.   34 *grace* favour.   35 *approve* prove, demonstrate.   36
plead my passions give evidence of my strong desires.   37 *Clubs* the cry of London

Full well shalt thou perceive how much I dare.

DEM.   Ay, boy, grow ye so brave?   *They draw.*

AAR.   Why, how now, lords?   45
So near the Emperor's palace dare ye draw
And maintain such a quarrel openly?
Full well I wot the ground of all this grudge.
I would not for a million of gold
The cause were known to them it most concerns;   50
Nor would your noble mother for much more
Be so dishonoured in the court of Rome.
For shame, put up!

DEM.   Not I, till I have sheath'd
My rapier in his bosom, and withal
Thrust those reproachful speeches down his throat   55
That he hath breath'd in my dishonour here.

CHI.   For that I am prepar'd and full resolv'd,
Foul-spoken coward, that thund'rest with thy tongue
And with thy weapon nothing dar'st perform.

AAR.   Away, I say!   60
Now, by the gods that warlike Goths adore,
This petty brabble will undo us all.
Why, lords, and think you not how dangerous
It is to jet upon a prince's right?
What, is Lavinia then become so loose,   65
Or Bassianus so degenerate,
That for her love such quarrels may be broach'd
Without controlment, justice, or revenge?
Young lords, beware! and should the Empress know

---

apprentices used to summon others to assist them in street fights, used generally
as a means of summoning the watch to stop brawls.   38 *unadvis'd* foolishly, without due consideration.   39 *dancing rapier* ornamental sword worn in dances.   40
desperate reckless.   41 *lath* sword of lath, traditionally carried by the Vice in medieval morality plays.   48 *wot* know.   54 *withal* at the same time.   62 *brabble*
brawl.   *undo* ruin.   64 *jet* encroach.   65 *loose* wanton, unchaste.   67 *broach'd*
set in motion; literally, "opened and set flowing," like a barrel of wine.   68 *controlment* restraint.

| | This discord's ground, the music would not please. | 70 |

CHI.   I care not, I, knew she and all the world.
I love Lavinia more than all the world.

DEM.   Youngling, learn thou to make some meaner choice.
Lavinia is thine elder brother's hope.

AAR.   Why, are ye mad? or know ye not, in Rome   75
How furious and impatient they be,
And cannot brook competitors in love?
I tell you, lords, you do but plot your deaths
By this device.

CHI.   Aaron, a thousand deaths
Would I propose to achieve her whom I love.   80

AAR.   To achieve her? How?

DEM.   Why makes thou it so strange?
She is a woman, therefore may be woo'd;
She is a woman, therefore may be won;
She is Lavinia, therefore must be lov'd.
What, man! More water glideth by the mill   85
Than wots the miller of; and easy it is
Of a cut loaf to steal a shive, we know.
Though Bassianus be the Emperor's brother,
Better than he have worn Vulcan's badge.

AAR.   [aside] Ay, and as good as Saturninus may.   90

DEM.   Then why should he despair that knows to court it
With words, fair looks, and liberality?
What, hast not thou full often stroke a doe,

---

70 *This discord's ground* the reason for this dissension. There is a pun on "ground" in its musical sense of the plain-song or bass background against which a descant is sung.   71 *knew she* if she knew.   73 *Youngling* youngster (a term of contempt). *meaner* of lower social status.   77 *brook* tolerate.   79 *device* enterprise. 80 *propose* be ready to encounter.   81 *makes thou* do you consider. This is common Elizabethan diction (Q¹; F¹, K: "mak'st thou").   85-6 *More water . . . miller of* A common proverb. *wots* knows.   87 *shive* slice.   89 *Vulcan's badge* the horns proverbially worn by the cuckold, the husband of an unfaithful wife. Vulcan was a cuckold because his wife, Venus, took Mars as a lover.   91 *to court it* how to court a woman.   93 *stroke* struck.   94 *cleanly* without being detected.   95 *snatch* quick, illicit sexual act.   96 *serve your turns* accomplish your purposes (with a

And borne her cleanly by the keeper's nose?

AAR.   Why, then it seems some certain snatch or so   95
       Would serve your turns.

CHI.   Ay, so the turn were serv'd.

DEM.   Aaron, thou hast hit it.

AAR.   Would you had hit it too!
       Then should not we be tir'd with this ado.
       Why, hark ye, hark ye! and are you such fools
       To square for this? Would it offend you then   100
       That both should speed?

CHI.   Faith, not me.

DEM.   Nor me, so I were one.   *That's the spirit!*

AAR.   For shame, be friends, and join for that you jar!
       'Tis policy and stratagem must do
       That you affect; and so must you resolve   105
       That what you cannot as you would achieve
       You must perforce accomplish as you may.
       Take this of me: Lucrece was not more chaste
       Than this Lavinia, Bassianus' love.
       A speedier course than ling'ring languishment   110
       Must we pursue, and I have found the path.
       My lords, a solemn hunting is in hand;
       There will the lovely Roman ladies troop.
       The forest walks are wide and spacious,
       And many unfrequented plots there are,   115
       Fitted by kind for rape and villainy.
       Single you thither then this dainty doe,

---

quibble, taken up in the next line, on "turn" in the sense of "sexual intercourse").
97 *hit it* hit the mark, guessed my meaning.   100 *square* come to blows.   101
speed be successful.   102 *so* so long as.   103 *join . . . jar* unite to obtain that
for which you are fighting.   104 *policy* cunning, trickery.   104–5 *do . . . affect*
accomplish what you desire.   105 *resolve* determine.   108 *Lucrece* the chaste
Roman matron whose rape by Tarquin and subsequent suicide are the subjects
of Shakespeare's poem, THE RAPE OF LUCRECE.   110 *than* ROWE; QQ, F¹: "this"
112 *solemn* ceremonial. *in hand* in progress.   114 *walks* paths.   115 *plots* places.
116 *Fitted by kind* adapted by nature.   117 *Single* select from the herd (a hunting
term).

And strike her home by force, if not by words.
This way, or not at all, stand you in hope.
Come, come, our Empress, with her sacred wit   120
To villainy and vengeance consecrate,
Will we acquaint withal what we intend;
And she shall file our engines with advice,
That will not suffer you to square yourselves,
But to your wishes' height advance you both.   125
The Emperor's court is like the House of Fame,
The palace full of tongues, of eyes and ears;
The woods are ruthless, dreadful, deaf, and dull.
There speak and strike, brave boys, and take your turns.
There serve your lust, shadowed from heaven's eye,   130
And revel in Lavinia's treasury.

CHI.   Thy counsel, lad, smells of no cowardice.

DEM.   *Sit fas aut nefas,* till I find the stream
         To cool this heat, a charm to calm these fits,
         Per Stygia, per manes vehor.   *Exeunt.* 135

◇◇◇◇◇◇◇◇◇◇◇◇◇◇◇◇◇◇

[SCENE II. *A forest near Rome.*]

Enter Titus Andronicus *and his three* Sons, [Martius,
    Lucius, *and* Quintus,] *making a noise with hounds
    and horns; and* Marcus.

TIT.   The hunt is up, the morn is bright and grey,
         The fields are fragrant, and the woods are green.
         Uncouple here, and let us make a bay,
         And wake the Emperor and his lovely bride,
         And rouse the Prince, and ring a hunter's peal,   5

---

119 *stand you in hope* is your only means of success.   120 *sacred* The word seems
to have little meaning here.   121 *consecrate* utterly devoted.   122 *withal* besides
(Q¹; к: "with all").   *what* with what (Q¹; F¹, к: "that").   123 *file our engines*
sharpen our wits.   124 *That* who, i.e. the Empress.   *suffer . . . yourselves* permit
you to fight with one another.   125 *to . . . height* to the ultimate of what you
desire.   126 *House of Fame* house of rumour. There may be an allusion to
Chaucer's poem of that name.   128 *ruthless* without pity.   130 *shadowed* shaded,

That all the court may echo with the noise.
Sons, let it be your charge, as it is ours,
To attend the Emperor's person carefully.
I have been troubled in my sleep this night,
But dawning day new comfort hath inspir'd.   10

> *Here a cry of hounds, and wind horns*
> *in a peal. Then enter* Saturninus, Ta-
> mora, Bassianus, Lavinia, Chiron, De-
> metrius, *and their* Attendants.

Many good morrows to your Majesty!
Madam, to you as many and as good!
I promised your Grace a hunter's peal.

SAT.   And you have rung it lustily, my lords,
Somewhat too early for new-married ladies.   15

BAS.   Lavinia, how say you?

LAV.   I say no.
I have been broad awake two hours and more.

SAT.   Come on then. Horse and chariots let us have,
And to our sport! [*To* Tamora] Madam, now
        shall ye see
Our Roman hunting.

MARC.   I have dogs, my lord,   20
Will rouse the proudest panther in the chase
And climb the highest promontory top.

TIT.   And I have horse will follow where the game
Makes way, and runs like swallows o'er the plain.

DEM.   Chiron, we hunt not, we, with horse nor hound,   25
But hope to pluck a dainty doe to ground.

                                Exeunt.

---

hidden.   133 *Sit . . . nefas* whether it be right or wrong.   135 *Per Stygia . . .*
vehor I am borne through the infernal (Stygian) regions. An adaptation from the
PHÆDRA of Seneca (line 1180). *Stygia* Q¹; F⁴, K: "Styga."
    II.II.   1 *up* ready.   *morn* F¹; Q¹: "Moone."   3 *Uncouple* let loose the hounds.
bay prolonged barking.   5 *peal* blowing of horns.   8 *attend* wait upon.   21 *chase*
hunting grounds.   24 *runs* Q¹; F², K: "run."

◇◇◇◇◇◇◇◇◇◇◇◇◇◇◇

[SCENE III. *A lonely part of the forest.*]

Enter Aaron *alone,* [*with a bag of gold*].

AAR. He that had wit would think that I had none
To bury so much gold under a tree
And never after to inherit it.
Let him that thinks of me so abjectly
Know that this gold must coin a stratagem,   5
Which, cunningly effected, will beget
A very excellent piece of villainy.
And so repose, sweet gold, for their unrest

[*Hides the gold.*]

That have their alms out of the Empress' chest.

Enter Tamora *alone, to the* Moor.

TAM. My lovely Aaron, wherefore look'st thou sad   10
When everything doth make a gleeful boast?
The birds chaunt melody on every bush;
The snake lies rolled in the cheerful sun;
The green leaves quiver with the cooling wind
And make a checker'd shadow on the ground.   15
Under their sweet shade, Aaron, let us sit,
And whilst the babbling echo mocks the hounds,
Replying shrilly to the well-tun'd horns,
As if a double hunt were heard at once,   *yelping*
Let us sit down and mark their yellowing noise;   20

II.iii.   3 *inherit* enjoy the possession of.   6 *beget* give birth to.   8–9 *for their . . . Empress' chest* to the ruin of those who find this gold which comes from the Empress' coffers.   11 *doth . . . boast* creates a joyful display.   13 *snake* Q²; Q¹: "snakes." *rolled* coiled up.   19 *hunt* sound of hunting.   20 *yellowing* yelping. An extension of "yell" by analogy with "bellow."   22 *The wand'ring prince* Æneas, the lover of Dido, Queen of Carthage. They recognized their passion for one another in a cave where they were driven by a storm.   23 *happy* fortunate. 24 *curtain'd with* shielded by. *counsel-keeping* secret-protecting.   26 *possess* enjoy.   30–1 *Venus . . . Saturn* Those born when the planet Venus was ascendant,

And — after conflict such as was suppos'd
The wand'ring prince and Dido once enjoy'd,
When with a happy storm they were surpris'd,
And curtain'd with a counsel-keeping cave —
We may, each wreathed in the other's arms   25
(Our pastimes done), possess a golden slumber,
Whiles hounds and horns and sweet melodious birds
Be unto us as is a nurse's song
Of lullaby to bring her babe asleep.

AAR.   Madam, though Venus govern your desires,   30
Saturn is dominator over mine.
What signifies my deadly-standing eye,
My silence, and my cloudy melancholy,
My fleece of woolly hair that now uncurls
Even as an adder when she doth unroll   35
To do some fatal execution?
No, madam, these are no Venereal signs.
Vengeance is in my heart, death in my hand,
Blood and revenge are hammering in my head.
Hark, Tamora, the empress of my soul,   40
Which never hopes more heaven than rests in thee —
This is the day of doom for Bassianus;
His Philomel must lose her tongue to-day,
Thy sons make pillage of her chastity
And wash their hands in Bassianus' blood.   45
Seest thou this letter? Take it up, I pray thee,
And give the King this fatal-plotted scroll.
Now question me no more. We are espied.
Here comes a parcel of our hopeful booty,
Which dreads not yet their lives' destruction.   50

---

and thus influenced by it throughout their lives, were of a lecherous disposition,
whereas those born under the influence of Saturn were sluggish, cold and gloomy
of temperament.   31 *dominator* the planet which dominates a man's life (an
astrological term).   32 *deadly-standing* fixed with a death-like glare.   37 *Venereal*
associated with Venus, goddess of love.   43 *Philomel* Philomela, whose tongue was
cut out by Tereus after he had raped her.   47 *fatal-plotted* planned for a deadly
purpose.   49 *parcel . . . booty* some of the victims we are expecting.   50 *Which
dreads not* who do not fear.

Enter Bassianus *and* Lavinia.

TAM.   Ah, my sweet Moor, sweeter to me than life!

AAR.   No more, great Empress. Bassianus comes.
         Be cross with him; and I'll go fetch thy sons
         To back thy quarrels, whatsoe'er they be.   [*Exit.*]

BAS.   Who have we here? Rome's royal Emperess,   55
         Unfurnish'd of her well-beseeming troop?
         Or is it Dian, habited like her,
         Who hath abandoned her holy groves
         To see the general hunting in this forest?

TAM.   Saucy controller of my private steps!   60
         Had I the power that some say Dian had,
         Thy temples should be planted presently
         With horns, as was Actæon's, and the hounds
         Should drive upon thy new-transformed limbs,
         Unmannerly intruder as thou art!   65

LAV.   Under your patience, gentle Emperess,
         'Tis thought you have a goodly gift in horning,
         And to be doubted that your Moor and you
         Are singled forth to try experiments.
         Jove shield your husband from his hounds to-day!   70
         'Tis pity they should take him for a stag.

BAS.   Believe me, Queen, your swarth Cimmerian
         Doth make your honour of his body's hue,
         Spotted, detested, and abominable.
         Why are you sequest'red from all your train,   75
         Dismounted from your snow-white goodly steed,

---

53 *Be cross* pick a quarrel.   54 *back* support.   56 *Unfurnish'd of* unaccompanied
by.   57 *Dian* Diana, goddess of chastity and the hunt.   *habited* dressed.   59
general public, common.   60 *Saucy controller* bitter critic.   63 *horns* the signs
of the cuckold.   *Actæon* a hunter who came upon Diana bathing in the forest.
She turned him into a stag, and he was torn to pieces by his own hounds.   66
Under your patience begging your pardon.   67 *goodly gift in* special talent for.
horning cuckolding a husband.   68 *doubted* suspected.   69 *Are singled forth*
have separated yourselves from the others.   *try experiments* experiment (Q²; Q¹:
"trie thy experimens").   71 *'Tis pity . . . a stag* it would be a pity if they were
to take him for a stag (since he would be wearing the horns of the cuckold).   72

And wand'red hither to an obscure plot,
Accompanied but with a barbarous Moor,
If foul desire had not conducted you?

LAV. And being intercepted in your sport,   80
Great reason that my noble lord be rated
For sauciness. — I pray you let us hence,
And let her joy her raven-coloured love.
This valley fits the purpose passing well.

BAS. The King my brother shall have notice of this.   85

LAV. Ay, for these slips have made him noted long.
Good king, to be so mightily abus'd!

TAM. Why have I patience to endure all this?

Enter Chiron *and* Demetrius.

DEM. How now, dear sovereign and our gracious mother?
Why doth your Highness look so pale and wan?   90

TAM. Have I not reason, think you, to look pale?
These two have 'tic'd me hither to this place.
A barren detested vale you see it is;
The trees, though summer, yet forlorn and lean,
O'ercome with moss and baleful mistletoe.   95
Here never shines the sun; here nothing breeds,
Unless the nightly owl or fatal raven.
And when they show'd me this abhorred pit,
They told me, here, at dead time of the night,
A thousand fiends, a thousand hissing snakes,   100
Ten thousand swelling toads, as many urchins,

---

swarth dark-complexioned (F¹; Q¹: "swartie"). *Cimmerian* one of a people believed to live in perpetual darkness.   74 *spotted* defiled.   75 *sequest'red* separated.   77 *obscure plot* deserted place.   81 *rated* berated.   83 *joy* enjoy.   84
passing exceedingly.   85 *notice* QQ, F¹; POPE, K: "note."   86 *noted* notorious.
long Of course, Bassianus has been only married for one night, but such com-
pression of time is not uncommon in Shakespeare.   87 *abus'd* deceived.   88 *have
I* F²; Q¹: "I haue," which may be correct if Tamora is regarded as speaking iron-
ically while plotting her revenge.   92 *'tic'd* enticed.   95 *O'ercome* overgrown.
baleful harmful, poisonous.   97 *owl . . . raven* traditionally regarded as birds of
ill omen.   101 *urchins* hedgehogs.

Would make such fearful and confused cries
As any mortal body hearing it
Should straight fall mad, or else die suddenly.
No sooner had they told this hellish tale   105
But straight they told me they would bind me here
Unto the body of a dismal yew
And leave me to this miserable death.
And then they call'd me foul adulteress,
Lascivious Goth, and all the bitterest terms   110
That ever ear did hear to such effect;
And had you not by wondrous fortune come,
This vengeance on me had they executed.
Revenge it, as you love your mother's life,
Or be ye not henceforth call'd my children.   115

DEM.   This is a witness that I am thy son.

                                        Stab [Bassianus].

CHI.   And this for me, struck home to show my strength.

                                        [*Stab him.*]

LAV.   Ay, come Semiramis — nay, barbarous Tamora!
        For no name fits thy nature but thy own!

TAM.   Give me the poniard. You shall know, my boys,   120
        Your mother's hand shall right your mother's wrong.

DEM.   Stay, madam! Here is more belongs to her.
        First thrash the corn, then after burn the straw.
        This minion stood upon her chastity,
        Upon her nuptial vow, her loyalty,   125
        And with that painted hope braves your mightiness;
        And shall she carry this unto her grave?

CHI.   An if she do, I would I were an eunuch.
        Drag hence her husband to some secret hole,

---

104 *straight* immediately. *suddenly* at once.   110 *Lascivious Goth* There is a
possible quibble on "goat," an animal proverbial for its lust.   112 *wondrous*
miraculous.   116 *a witness* evidence.   118 *Semiramis* Cf. II.I. 22.   120 *poniard*
dagger.   124 *minion* saucy contemptible creature.   *stood upon* made a great issue
of.   126 *painted* false, specious.   *braves* affronts, insults.   127 *carry this* continue
in this manner.   130 *trunk* body.   131 *we desire* Tamora enters wholeheartedly

| | And make his dead trunk pillow to our lust. | 130 |

TAM.   But when ye have the honey we desire,
Let not this wasp outlive, us both to sting.

CHI.   I warrant you, madam, we will make that sure.
Come, mistress, now perforce we will enjoy
That nice-preserved honesty of yours.   135

LAV.   O Tamora! thou bearest a woman's face —

TAM.   I will not hear her speak. Away with her!

LAV.   Sweet lords, entreat her hear me but a word.

DEM.   Listen, fair madam. Let it be your glory
To see her tears; but be your heart to them   140
As unrelenting flint to drops of rain.

LAV.   When did the tiger's young ones teach the dam?
O, do not learn her wrath! She taught it thee;
The milk thou suck'st from her did turn to marble;
Even at thy teat thou hadst thy tyranny.   145
Yet every mother breeds not sons alike.
[*To* Chiron] Do thou entreat her show a woman's pity.

CHI.   What, wouldst thou have me prove myself a bastard?

LAV.   'Tis true — the raven doth not hatch a lark.
Yet have I heard (O, could I find it now!)   150
The lion, mov'd with pity, did endure
To have his princely paws par'd all away.
Some say that ravens foster forlorn children
The whilst their own birds famish in their nests.
O, be to me, though thy hard heart say no,   155
Nothing so kind, but something pitiful!

TAM.   I know not what it means. Away with her!

LAV.   O, let me teach thee! For my father's sake,

---

into the desires of her sons (Q¹; F², K: "ye desire").   132 *outlive* survive.   134
perforce by force.   135 *nice-preserved* carefully preserved. *honesty* chastity.   142
dam mother.   143 *learn* teach.   144 *suck'st* Q¹; ROWE, K: "suck'dst."   150 *find it*
discover it to be true.   153 *forlorn* abandoned.   154 *The whilst* while. *birds*
young birds. *famish* starve.   156 *Nothing . . . pitiful* not so kind as that (as the
raven) but showing at least some pity.   157 *it* pity.

That gave thee life when well he might have slain thee,
Be not obdurate, open thy deaf ears.   160

TAM.   Hadst thou in person ne'er offended me,
        Even for his sake am I pitiless.
        Remember, boys, I pour'd forth tears in vain
        To save your brother from the sacrifice;
        But fierce Andronicus would not relent.   165
        Therefore away with her, and use her as you will;
        The worse to her, the better lov'd of me.

LAV.   O Tamora, be call'd a gentle queen
        And with thine own hands kill me in this place!
        For 'tis not life that I have begg'd so long.   170
        Poor I was slain when Bassianus died.

TAM.   What begg'st thou then? Fond woman, let me go.

LAV.   'Tis present death I beg; and one thing more
        That womanhood denies my tongue to tell:
        O, keep me from their worse than killing lust,   175
        And tumble me into some loathsome pit,
        Where never man's eye may behold my body.
        Do this, and be a charitable murderer.

TAM.   So should I rob my sweet sons of their fee.
        No, let them satisfy their lust on thee.   180

DEM.   Away! for thou hast stay'd us here too long.

LAV.   No grace? no womanhood? Ah, beastly creature,
        The blot and enemy to our general name!
        Confusion fall —

CHI.   Nay then, I'll stop your mouth. — Bring thou her
                husband.   185
        This is the hole where Aaron bid us hide him.

            [Demetrius *throws the body of* Bassi-
            anus *into the pit; then exeunt* Deme-

---

160 *ears* Q³; Q¹: "yeares."   167 *The worse . . . of me* the worse you treat her the
more I will love you.   172 *Fond* foolish.   173 *present* immediate.   174 *denies*
does not permit.   181 *stay'd* detained.   183 *our general name* the name of all
women.   187 *make her sure* see that she is completely taken care of.   191 *spleen-*

trius *and* Chiron, *dragging off* Lavinia.]

TAM. Farewell, my sons. See that you make her sure. *into the cave with her!*
Ne'er let my heart know merry cheer indeed
Till all the Andronici be made away.
Now will I hence to seek my lovely Moor   190
And let my spleenful sons this trull deflow'r.   *Exit.*

Enter Aaron, *with two of* Titus' Sons,
[Quintus *and* Martius].

AAR. Come on, my lords; the better foot before.
Straight will I bring you to the loathsome pit
Where I espied the panther fast asleep.

QUINT. My sight is very dull, whate'er it bodes.   195

MART. And mine, I promise you. Were it not for shame,
Well could I leave our sport to sleep awhile.

[*Falls into the pit.*]

QUINT. What, art thou fallen? What subtile hole is this,
Whose mouth is covered with rude-growing briers,
Upon whose leaves are drops of new-shed blood   200
As fresh as morning dew distill'd on flowers?
A very fatal place it seems to me.
Speak, brother. Hast thou hurt thee with the fall?

MART. O brother, with the dismall'st object hurt
That ever eye with sight made heart lament!   205

AAR. [*aside*] Now will I fetch the King to find them here,
That he thereby may have a likely guess
How these were they that made away his brother.
Exit.

MART. Why dost not comfort me and help me out

---

ful angry, lustful. The spleen was regarded as a source of the passions.   *trull*
harlot.   193 *Straight* immediately.   *bring* conduct.   195 *My sight . . . it bodes*
I cannot see very well, whatever evil that may foretell.   196 *promise* assure.   198
subtile treacherous.   202 *fatal* ill-omened.   204 *with* by.

	From this unhallowed and blood-stained hole?	210
QUINT.	I am surprised with an uncouth fear;	
	A chilling sweat o'erruns my trembling joints;	
	My heart suspects more than mine eye can see.	
MART.	To prove thou hast a true-divining heart,	
	Aaron and thou look down into this den	215
	And see a fearful sight of blood and death.	
QUINT.	Aaron is gone, and my compassionate heart	
	Will not permit mine eyes once to behold	
	The thing whereat it trembles by surmise.	
	O, tell me who it is! for ne'er till now	220
	Was I a child to fear I know not what.	
MART.	Lord Bassianus lies beray'd in blood,	
	All on a heap, like to a slaughtered lamb,	
	In this detested, dark, blood-drinking pit.	
QUINT.	If it be dark, how dost thou know 'tis he?	225
MART.	Upon his bloody finger he doth wear	
	A precious ring that lightens all this hole,	
	Which, like a taper in some monument,	
	Doth shine upon the dead man's earthy cheeks	
	And shows the ragged entrails of the pit.	230
	So pale did shine the moon on Pyramus	
	When he by night lay bath'd in maiden blood.	
	O brother, help me with thy fainting hand	
	(If fear hath made thee faint, as me it hath)	
	Out of this fell devouring receptacle,	235
	As hateful as Cocytus' misty mouth.	
QUINT.	Reach me thy hand, that I may help thee out,	
	Or, wanting strength to do thee so much good,	

---

210 *unhallowed* F¹; Q¹: "vnhollow." 211 *surprised* overcome. *uncouth* strange, uncanny. 217 *compassionate* sympathetic, full of natural feeling. 219 *whereat . . . surmise* at which it quakes merely to imagine. 221 *a child . . . not what* so childish as to fear the unknown. 222 *beray'd in blood* WILSON; Q¹: "bereaud in blood"; Q²⁻³, F¹, K: "embrewed heere." *beray'd* fouled, defiled. 223 *on a heap* prostrate. 228 *taper* candle. *monument* tomb. 230 *ragged entrails* rough interior. 231 *Pyramus* the lover of Thisbe, who killed himself in the belief that

I may be pluck'd into the swallowing womb
Of this deep pit, poor Bassianus' grave.   240
I have no strength to pluck thee to the brink.

MART.   Nor I no strength to climb without thy help.

QUINT.   Thy hand once more! I will not loose again
Till thou art here aloft, or I below.
Thou canst not come to me — I come to thee.   245

Both fall in.

Enter the Emperor [Saturninus] *and*
Aaron *the Moor.*

SAT.   Along with me! I'll see what hole is here
And what he is that now is leapt into it.
Say, who art thou that lately didst descend
Into this gaping hollow of the earth?

MART.   The unhappy sons of old Andronicus,   250
Brought hither in a most unlucky hour
To find thy brother Bassianus dead.

SAT.   My brother dead? I know thou dost but jest.
He and his lady both are at the lodge
Upon the north side of this pleasant chase.   255
'Tis not an hour since I left them there.

MART.   We know not where you left them all alive;
But, out alas! here have we found him dead.

Enter Tamora [*with* Attendants;
Titus] Andronicus, *and* Lucius.

TAM.   Where is my lord the King?

SAT.   Here, Tamora; though griev'd with killing grief.   260

she was dead (Q²; Q¹: "Priamus").   232 *maiden blood* the blood of virgin lovers.
235 *fell* savage, cruel.   *receptacle* tomb.   236 *Cocytus* one of the four rivers of
the classical Hades, here used for Hell itself (F²; QQ, F¹: "Ocitus").   238 *wanting*
lacking.   239 *pluck'd* pulled.   243 *loose* let go.   246 *Along* come along.   247
what who.   250 *unhappy* unfortunate.   *sons* Q¹: Q², K: "sonne."   254 *lodge* hunting lodge.   255 *chase* hunting ground.

TAM.	Where is thy brother Bassianus?
SAT.	Now to the bottom dost thou search my wound.
	Poor Bassianus here lies murdered.
TAM.	Then all too late I bring this fatal writ,
	The complot of this timeless tragedy; 265
	And wonder greatly that man's face can fold
	In pleasing smiles such murderous tyranny.

She giveth Saturnine *a letter.*
Saturninus *reads the letter.*

"An if we miss to meet him handsomely,
Sweet huntsman — Bassianus 'tis we mean —
Do thou so much as dig the grave for him.   270
Thou know'st our meaning. Look for thy reward
Among the nettles at the elder tree
Which overshades the mouth of that same pit
Where we decreed to bury Bassianus.
Do this, and purchase us thy lasting friends."   275

SAT.	O Tamora! was ever heard the like?
	This is the pit, and this the elder tree.
	Look, sirs, if you can find the huntsman out
	That should have murdered Bassianus here.
AAR.	My gracious lord, here is the bag of gold. 280
SAT.	[*To* Titus] Two of thy whelps, fell curs of bloody kind,
	Have here bereft my brother of his life. —
	Sirs, drag them from the pit unto the prison.
	There let them bide until we have devis'd
	Some never-heard-of torturing pain for them. 285
TAM.	What, are they in this pit? O wondrous thing!
	How easily murder is discovered!
TIT.	High Emperor, upon my feeble knee
	I beg this boon, with tears not lightly shed,

---

262 *search* probe.   265 *complot* plot.   *timeless* untimely.   266 *fold* enfold, conceal.   268 *handsomely* conveniently.   271 *meaning* intentions.   275 *purchase us* win us as.   *lasting* eternal.   279 *should have* was to have.   281 *kind* nature.   282 *bereft* deprived.   287 *discovered* revealed.   290 *fell fault* savage crime.   291

	That this fell fault of my accursed sons —	290
	Accursed if the fault be prov'd in them —	
SAT.	If it be prov'd? You see it is apparent.	
	Who found this letter? Tamora, was it you?	
TAM.	Andronicus himself did take it up.	
TIT.	I did, my lord. Yet let me be their bail;	295
	For by my father's reverent tomb I vow	
	They shall be ready at your Highness' will	
	To answer their suspicion with their lives.	
SAT.	Thou shalt not bail them. See thou follow me.	
	Some bring the murdered body, some the murderers.	300
	Let them not speak a word — the guilt is plain;	
	For, by my soul, were there worse end than death,	
	That end upon them should be executed.	
TAM.	Andronicus, I will entreat the King.	
	Fear not thy sons; they shall do well enough.	305
TIT.	Come, Lucius, come! Stay not to talk with them.	

Exeunt.

◇◇◇◇◇◇◇◇◇◇◇◇◇◇◇◇◇

[SCENE IV. *Another part of the forest.*]

Enter the Empress' Sons, [Demetrius *and* Chiron,] *with*
    Lavinia, *her hands cut off, and her tongue cut out,*
    and ravish'd.

DEM.	So, now go tell, an if thy tongue can speak,
	Who 'twas that cut thy tongue and ravish'd thee.
CHI.	Write down thy mind, bewray thy meaning so,

---

fault THEOBALD; QQ, F¹: "faults."   292 *apparent* obvious.   298 *answer their sus-*
picion pay for the crime of which they are suspected.   305 *Fear not* do not be
afraid for. *do well* (a) come out all right (b) die — a common euphemism.
   II.IV. 3 *bewray* reveal.

An if thy stumps will let thee play the scribe.

DEM.   See how with signs and tokens she can scrowl.   5

CHI.   Go home, call for sweet water, wash thy hands.

DEM.   She hath no tongue to call, nor hands to wash;
And so let's leave her to her silent walks.

CHI.   An 'twere my cause, I should go hang myself.

DEM.   If thou hadst hands to help thee knit the cord.   10

Exeunt [Demetrius *and* Chiron].

Wind horns. Enter Marcus, *from
hunting.*

MAR.   Who is this? — my niece, that flies away so fast?
Cousin, a word. Where is your husband?
If I do dream, would all my wealth would wake me!
If I do wake, some planet strike me down,
That I may slumber an eternal sleep!   15
Speak, gentle niece. What stern ungentle hands
Hath lopp'd and hew'd and made thy body bare
Of her two branches — those sweet ornaments
Whose circling shadows kings have sought to sleep in
And might not gain so great a happiness   20
As half thy love? Why dost not speak to me?
Alas, a crimson river of warm blood,
Like to a bubbling fountain stirr'd with wind,
Doth rise and fall between thy rosed lips,
Coming and going with thy honey breath.   25
But sure some Tereus hath deflow'red thee,
And lest thou shouldst detect him, cut thy tongue.

---

5 *scrowl* scrawl, write.   6 *sweet water* perfume.   9 *cause* case, situation.   10 *knit*
tie.   12 *Cousin* kinswoman.   14 *do wake* am awake.   *planet . . . down* It was
believed that evil planets could strike men with their rays (influence) and drive
them mad or kill them.   16 *hands* Q¹; K: "hand."   17–18 *hath lopp'd . . .
branches* The imagery is from the pruning of trees.   26 *Tereus* the ravisher of
Philomela.   27 *detect* expose.   30 *three* HANMER; QQ, F¹: "their."   31 *Titan* the
sun god.   32 *with* by.   34 *thy heart* what is in your mind. The heart was a
centre of thought as well as emotion.   36 *oven stopp'd* Elizabethan ovens were

Ah, now thou turn'st away thy face for shame!
And, notwithstanding all this loss of blood,
As from a conduit with three issuing spouts,   30
Yet do thy cheeks look red as Titan's face
Blushing to be encoun'tred with a cloud.
Shall I speak for thee? Shall I say 'tis so?
O that I knew thy heart! and knew the beast,
That I might rail at him to ease my mind!   35
Sorrow concealed, like an oven stopp'd,
Doth burn the heart to cinders where it is.
Fair Philomel — why, she but lost her tongue,
And in a tedious sampler sew'd her mind;
But, lovely niece, that mean is cut from thee.   40
A craftier Tereus, cousin, hast thou met,
And he hath cut those pretty fingers off
That could have better sew'd than Philomel.
O, had the monster seen those lily hands
Tremble like aspen leaves upon a lute   45
And make the silken strings delight to kiss them,
He would not then have touch'd them for his life!
Or had he heard the heavenly harmony
Which that sweet tongue hath made,
He would have dropp'd his knife, and fell asleep,   50
As Cerberus at the Thracian poet's feet.
Come, let us go and make thy father blind;
For such a sight will blind a father's eye.
One hour's storm will drown the fragrant meads;
What will whole months of tears thy father's eyes?   55
Do not draw back, for we will mourn with thee.
O, could our mourning ease thy misery!

Exeunt.

---

sealed after food had been placed in them to be cooked. Unless the oven was
opened in time, the food would burn.   39 *And in . . . her mind* Philomela
sewed the story of her rape by Tereus into a tapestry. *tedious* laboriously executed. *sew'd* POPE; QQ, F¹: "sowed." *mind* thoughts.   40 *mean* means.   43 *sew'd*
POPE; QQ, F¹: "sowed."   51 *As Cerberus . . . feet* When Orpheus (the Thracian
poet) came to the underworld to seek Eurydice among the dead, the music of his
lute charmed Cerberus, the three-headed dog who guarded the entrance to Hades.

Act Three

[SCENE I. *Rome. A street.*]

Enter the Judges, [Tribunes,] *and* Senators, *with* Titus'
two Sons, [Martius *and* Quintus,] *bound, passing on
the stage to the place of execution, and* Titus *going
before, pleading.*

TIT. Hear me, grave fathers — noble Tribunes, stay,
For pity of mine age, whose youth was spent
In dangerous wars whilst you securely slept.
For all my blood in Rome's great quarrel shed,
For all the frosty nights that I have watch'd,   5
And for these bitter tears which now you see
Filling the aged wrinkles in my cheeks,
Be pitiful to my condemned sons,
Whose souls are not corrupted as 'tis thought.
For two-and-twenty sons I never wept,   10
Because they died in honour's lofty bed.

> Andronicus *lieth down, and the* Judges
> [*etc.*] *pass by him* [*with the prisoners
> and exeunt*].

For these, Tribunes, in the dust I write

III.I. 5 *watch'd* gone without sleep. 11 *s.d. lieth down* He probably throws himself prostrate on the ground. 13 *languor* anguish. 14 *stanch* satisfy. 17 *distil*
pour out. *urns* i.e. his eyes (HANMER; QQ, F¹: "ruines"). 19 *still* constantly. 22
So so long as. 23 *gentle* noble. 24 *doom* judgment. 25 *that* who. 26 *orators*

42

My heart's deep languor and my soul's sad tears.
Let my tears stanch the earth's dry appetite.
My sons' sweet blood will make it shame and blush.   15
O earth, I will befriend thee more with rain
That shall distil from these two ancient urns
Than youthful April shall with all his show'rs.
In summer's drought I'll drop upon thee still,
In winter with warm tears I'll melt the snow,   20
And keep eternal springtime on thy face,
So thou refuse to drink my dear sons' blood.

                Enter Lucius, *with his weapon drawn.*

O reverent Tribunes, O gentle aged men,
Unbind my sons, reverse the doom of death;
And let me say (that never wept before)   25
My tears are now prevailing orators!

LUC.   O noble father, you lament in vain.
The Tribunes hear you not; no man is by,
And you recount your sorrows to a stone.

TIT.   Ah, Lucius, for thy brothers let me plead.   30
Grave Tribunes, once more I entreat of you —

LUC.   My gracious lord, no tribune hears you speak.

TIT.   Why, 'tis no matter, man. If they did hear,
They would not mark me; or if they did mark,
They would not pity me. Yet plead I must;   35
And bootless unto them.
Therefore I tell my sorrows to the stones;
Who, though they cannot answer my distress,
Yet in some sort they are better than the Tribunes,
For that they will not intercept my tale.   40
When I do weep, they humbly at my feet
Receive my tears and seem to weep with me;
And were they but attired in grave weeds,

---

pleaders.   28 *by* present.   34 *mark* pay attention to. *or* Q²; F¹: "oh"; not in Q¹.
36 *bootless* in vain.   39 *sort* respect.   40 *For that* because. *intercept* interrupt.
43 *grave weeds* solemn garments.

Rome could afford no tribune like to these.
A stone is soft as wax, tribunes more hard than stones.   45
A stone is silent and offendeth not,
And tribunes with their tongues doom men to death.

                              [*Rises.*]

But wherefore stand'st thou with thy weapon drawn?

LUC.   To rescue my two brothers from their death;
         For which attempt the judges have pronounc'd   50
         My everlasting doom of banishment.

TIT.   O happy man! they have befriended thee.
         Why, foolish Lucius, dost thou not perceive
         That Rome is but a wilderness of tigers?
         Tigers must prey, and Rome affords no prey   55
         But me and mine. How happy art thou then
         From these devourers to be banished!
         But who comes with our brother Marcus here?

                    Enter Marcus *with* Lavinia.

MARC.   Titus, prepare thy aged eyes to weep,
         Or if not so, thy noble heart to break.   60
         I bring consuming sorrow to thine age.

TIT.   Will it consume me? Let me see it then.

MARC.   This was thy daughter.

TIT.   Why, Marcus, so she is.

LUC.   Ay me, this object kills me!

TIT.   Faint-hearted boy, arise and look upon her.   65
         Speak, Lavinia, what accursed hand
         Hath made thee handless in thy father's sight?
         What fool hath added water to the sea

---

51 *everlasting doom of* sentence of everlasting.   56 *mine* my family. *happy* fortunate.   64 *object* sight.   71 *Nilus* the river Nile. *disdaineth bounds* has no
respect for what should contain and restrict it.   75 *bootless* vain.   76 *to effectless
use* for ineffectual purposes.   81 *martyr'd* mutilated.   82 *engine of* instrument for
expressing.   83 *blabb'd* freely uttered.   87 *say* speak.   88 *park* deer park.   90

Or brought a fagot to bright-burning Troy?
My grief was at the height before thou cam'st,   70
And now like Nilus it disdaineth bounds.
Give me a sword! I'll chop off my hands too;
For they have fought for Rome, and all in vain;
And they have nurs'd this woe in feeding life;
In bootless prayer have they been held up,   75
And they have serv'd me to effectless use.
Now all the service I require of them
Is that the one will help to cut the other.
'Tis well, Lavinia, that thou hast no hands;
For hands to do Rome service, is but vain.   80

LUC.   Speak, gentle sister. Who hath martyr'd thee?

MARC.   O, that delightful engine of her thoughts
That blabb'd them with such pleasing eloquence
Is torn from forth that pretty hollow cage
Where, like a sweet melodious bird, it sung   85
Sweet varied notes, enchanting every ear!

LUC.   O, say thou for her! Who hath done this deed?

MARC.   O, thus I found her straying in the park,
Seeking to hide herself as doth the deer
That hath receiv'd some unrecuring wound.   90

TIT.   It was my dear, and he that wounded her
Hath hurt me more than had he kill'd me dead;
For now I stand as one upon a rock,
Environ'd with a wilderness of sea,
Who marks the waxing tide grow wave by wave,   95
Expecting ever when some envious surge
Will in his brinish bowels swallow him.
This way to death my wretched sons are gone;
Here stands my other son, a banish'd man,
And here my brother, weeping at my woes.   100

---

unrecuring wound wound which cannot be healed.   91 *my dear* The pun on
"deer" is very common in Shakespeare.   94 *Environ'd* surrounded. *wilderness*
wild waste.   96 *Expecting . . . when* always waiting for the time when. *envious*
malicious, spiteful.   97 *his* its. *brinish* salty.

But that which gives my soul the greatest spurn
Is dear Lavinia, dearer than my soul.
Had I but seen thy picture in this plight,
It would have madded me. What shall I do
Now I behold thy lively body so?   105
Thou hast no hands to wipe away thy tears,
Nor tongue to tell me who hath martyr'd thee.
Thy husband he is dead, and for his death
Thy brothers are condemn'd, and dead by this.
Look, Marcus! Ah, son Lucius, look on her!   110
When I did name her brothers, then fresh tears
Stood on her cheeks, as doth the honey-dew
Upon a gath'red lily almost withered.

MARC. Perchance she weeps because they kill'd her husband;
       Perchance because she knows them innocent.   115

TIT. If they did kill thy husband, then be joyful,
      Because the law hath ta'en revenge on them.
No, no! they would not do so foul a deed;
Witness the sorrow that their sister makes.
Gentle Lavinia, let me kiss thy lips,   120
Or make some sign how I may do thee ease.
Shall thy good uncle and thy brother Lucius
And thou and I sit round about some fountain,
Looking all downwards to behold our cheeks
How they are stain'd, like meadows yet not dry   125
With miry slime left on them by a flood?
And in the fountain shall we gaze so long
Till the fresh taste be taken from that clearness,
And made a brine-pit with our bitter tears?
Or shall we cut away our hands like thine?   130
Or shall we bite our tongues, and in dumb shows
Pass the remainder of our hateful days?
What shall we do? Let us that have our tongues
Plot some device of further misery,

---

101 *spurn* contemptuous stroke. 105 *lively* living. 107 *martyr'd* mutilated. 109 *by this* by this time. 112 *honey-dew* sweet dew. 121 *do thee ease* help you. 128 *that clearness* the clarity of the fountain. 129 *And made* and it be turned into. *with* by. 131 *in dumb shows* in making speechless signs. 139 *wot* know.

	To make us wond'red at in time to come.	135
LUC.	Sweet father, cease your tears; for at your grief	
	See how my wretched sister sobs and weeps.	
MARC.	Patience, dear niece. Good Titus, dry thine eyes.	
TIT.	Ah, Marcus, Marcus! Brother, well I wot	
	Thy napkin cannot drink a tear of mine,	140
	For thou, poor man, hast drown'd it with thine own.	
LUC.	Ah, my Lavinia, I will wipe thy cheeks.	
TIT.	Mark, Marcus, mark! I understand her signs.	
	Had she a tongue to speak, now would she say	
	That to her brother which I said to thee.	145
	His napkin, with his true tears all bewet,	
	Can do no service on her sorrowful cheeks.	
	O, what a sympathy of woe is this —	
	As far from help as Limbo is from bliss!	

Enter Aaron the Moor.

AAR.	Titus Andronicus, my lord the Emperor	150
	Sends thee this word, that, if thou love thy sons,	
	Let Marcus, Lucius, or thyself, old Titus,	
	Or any one of you, chop off your hand	
	And send it to the King: he for the same	
	Will send thee hither both thy sons alive;	155
	And that shall be the ransom for their fault.	
TIT.	O gracious Emperor! O gentle Aaron!	
	Did ever raven sing so like a lark	
	That gives sweet tidings of the sun's uprise?	
	With all my heart I'll send the Emperor my hand.	160
	Good Aaron, wilt thou help to chop it off?	
LUC.	Stay, father! for that noble hand of thine,	
	That hath thrown down so many enemies,	

---

140 *napkin* handkerchief.   146 *with his* F⁴; QQ, F¹: "with her." *bewet* soaked.
148 *sympathy* agreement, affinity.   149 *Limbo* a place near Hell reserved for those unworthy of damnation but incapable of entering heaven through no fault of their own.

Shall not be sent. My hand will serve the turn.
My youth can better spare my blood than you,   165
And therefore mine shall save my brothers' lives.

MARC.   Which of your hands hath not defended Rome
And rear'd aloft the bloody battleaxe,
Writing destruction on the enemy's castle?
O, none of both but are of high desert!   170
My hand hath been but idle; let it serve
To ransom my two nephews from their death.
Then have I kept it to a worthy end.

AAR.   Nay, come, agree whose hand shall go along,
For fear they die before their pardon come.   175

MARC.   My hand shall go.

LUC.   By heaven, it shall not go!

TIT.   Sirs, strive no more. Such with'red herbs as these
Are meet for plucking up, and therefore mine!

LUC.   Sweet father, if I shall be thought thy son,
Let me redeem my brothers both from death.   180

MARC.   And for our father's sake and mother's care,
Now let me show a brother's love to thee.

TIT.   Agree between you. I will spare my hand.

LUC.   Then I'll go fetch an axe.

MARC.   But I will use the axe.   *Exeunt* [Lucius *and* Marcus]. 185

TIT.   Come hither, Aaron. I'll deceive them both.
Lend me thy hand, and I will give thee mine.

AAR.   [*aside*] If that be call'd deceit, I will be honest
And never whilst I live deceive men so.
But I'll deceive you in another sort,   190

---

173 *to* for.   178 *meet* fit.   179 *shall be* am to be.   190 *sort* way.   192 *stay your strife* stop your argument. *is dispatch'd* has been taken care of.   194 *warded* protected.   197 *account of* consider.   201 *Look* expect.   203 *fat me* make me happy (literally, "nourish me").   204 *fair* light-complexioned.   207 *this feeble ruin* i.e. his body.   211 *breathe . . . dim* make the sky (welkin) cloudy with our

And that you'll say ere half an hour pass.

He cuts off Titus' *hand.*

Enter Lucius *and* Marcus *again.*

TIT.   Now stay your strife. What shall be is dispatch'd.
        Good Aaron, give his Majesty my hand.
        Tell him it was a hand that warded him
        From thousand dangers; bid him bury it.   195
        More hath it merited — that let it have.
        As for my sons, say I account of them
        As jewels purchas'd at an easy price;
        And yet dear too, because I bought mine own.

AAR.   I go, Andronicus; and for thy hand   200
        Look by-and-by to have thy sons with thee.
        [*Aside*] Their heads, I mean. O, how this villainy
        Doth fat me with the very thoughts of it!
        Let fools do good, and fair men call for grace,
        Aaron will have his soul black like his face.   *Exit.* 205

TIT.   O, here I lift this one hand up to heaven
        And bow this feeble ruin to the earth.
        If any power pities wretched tears,
        To that I call! — [*To* Lavinia] What, wouldst thou kneel
              with me?
        Do then, dear heart; for heaven shall hear our prayers,   210
        Or with our sighs we'll breathe the welkin dim
        And stain the sun with fog, as sometime clouds
        When they do hug him in their melting bosoms.

MARC.   O brother, speak with possibility,
        And do not break into these deep extremes.   215

TIT.   Is not my sorrow deep, having no bottom?
        Then be my passions bottomless with them!

MARC.   But yet let reason govern thy lament.

breath (words).   212 *sometime* sometimes.   213 *him* the sun.   214 *with possi-*
bility of things which are possible.   215 *break . . . extremes* engage in such ex-
travagant talk.   217 *passions* passionate cries.   *bottomless* infinite in scope.   218
lament lamentations.

TIT. If there were reason for these miseries,
 Then into limits could I bind my woes. 220
 When heaven doth weep, doth not the earth o'erflow?
 If the winds rage, doth not the sea wax mad,
 Threat'ning the welkin with his big-swol'n face?
 And wilt thou have a reason for this coil?
 I am the sea; hark how her sighs doth blow! 225
 She is the weeping welkin, I the earth:
 Then must my sea be moved with her sighs;
 Then must my earth with her continual tears
 Become a deluge, overflow'd and drown'd;
 For why my bowels cannot hide her woes, 230
 But like a drunkard must I vomit them.
 Then give me leave; for losers will have leave
 To ease their stomachs with their bitter tongues.

Enter a Messenger, *with two heads and a hand.*

MESS. Worthy Andronicus, ill art thou repaid
 For that good hand thou sent'st the Emperor. 235
 Here are the heads of thy two noble sons;
 And here's thy hand, in scorn to thee sent back —
 Thy grief their sports, thy resolution mock'd,
 That woe is me to think upon thy woes
 More than remembrance of my father's death. *Exit.* 240

MARC. Now let hot Ætna cool in Sicily,
 And be my heart an ever-burning hell!
 These miseries are more than may be borne.
 To weep with them that weep doth ease some deal;
 But sorrow flouted at is double death. 245

---

220 *into limits . . . woes* I would confine my sorrows within reasonable bounds.
222 *wax* grow. 223 *welkin* sky. 224 *coil* turmoil, disturbance. 225 *doth* Q¹;
F¹, K: "do." *blow* F²; QQ, F¹: "flow," which could be correct in the sense of "issue
forth," although it is rejected by most editors. 227 *with* by. 230 *For why*
because. *bowels* sources of compassion. *hide* contain, keep within them. 233
ease their stomachs relieve their passions. The stomach was regarded as one of
the organs where passions originated. 234 *ill* badly. 238 *their sports* a source
of amusement to them. *resolution* resolute action. 239–40 *That woe . . . death*
so that it is a greater sorrow for me to think of your sorrows than it is for me

LUC.   Ah, that this sight should make so deep a wound
        And yet detested life not shrink thereat!
        That ever death should let life bear his name
        Where life hath no more interest but to breathe!

                              [Lavinia *kisses* Titus.]

MARC.   Alas, poor heart! that kiss is comfortless   250
        As frozen water to a starved snake.

TIT.   When will this fearful slumber have an end?

MARC.   Now farewell, flatt'ry; die, Andronicus.
        Thou dost not slumber. See thy two sons' heads,
        Thy warlike hand, thy mangled daughter here,   255
        Thy other banish'd son with this dear sight
        Struck pale and bloodless, and thy brother, I,
        Even like a stony image, cold and numb.
        Ah, now no more will I control thy griefs!
        Rent off thy silver hair, thy other hand   260
        Gnawing with thy teeth; and be this dismal sight
        The closing up of our most wretched eyes.
        Now is a time to storm. Why art thou still?

TIT.   Ha, ha, ha!

MARC.   Why dost thou laugh? It fits not with this hour.   265

TIT.   Why, I have not another tear to shed.
        Besides, this sorrow is an enemy,
        And would usurp upon my wat'ry eyes
        And make them blind with tributary tears.
        Then which way shall I find Revenge's cave?   270
        For these two heads do seem to speak to me,

---

to mourn the death of my father.   241 *Ætna* a volcano in Sicily.   244 *ease some
deal* provide some relief.   245 *flouted at* mocked.   247 *shrink* slip away.   248
bear his name continue to be called life.   249 *hath no . . . breathe* consists of no
more than mere breathing.   251 *starved* benumbed with cold.   252 *fearful* dreadful, frightening.   *slumber* dream.   256 *dear* dire, painful.   259 *griefs* lamentations.   260 *Rent* rend, tear.   262 *The closing . . . eyes* i.e. our deaths.   268
usurp upon capture, take control of.   269 *tributary tears* tears paid as tribute to
the hostile captor, sorrow.

And threat me I shall never come to bliss
Till all these mischiefs be return'd again
Even in their throats that hath committed them.
Come, let me see what task I have to do.   275
You heavy people, circle me about,
That I may turn me to each one of you
And swear unto my soul to right your wrongs.
The vow is made. Come, brother, take a head;
And in this hand the other will I bear.   280
Lavinia, thou shalt be employ'd in these things.
Bear thou my hand, sweet wench, between thy teeth.
As for thee, boy, go get thee from my sight!
Thou art an exile, and thou must not stay.
Hie to the Goths and raise an army there;   285
And if ye love me, as I think you do,
Let's kiss and part, for we have much to do.

                              Exeunt. Manet Lucius.

LUC.   Farewell, Andronicus, my noble father,
       The woefull'st man that ever liv'd in Rome.
       Farewell, proud Rome, till Lucius come again!   290
       He leaves his pledges dearer than his life.
       Farewell, Lavinia, my noble sister.
       O, would thou wert as thou tofore hast been!
       But now nor Lucius nor Lavinia lives
       But in oblivion and hateful griefs.   295
       If Lucius live, he will requite your wrongs
       And make proud Saturnine and his emperess
       Beg at the gates like Tarquin and his queen.
       Now will I to the Goths and raise a pow'r,
       To be reveng'd on Rome and Saturnine.   *Exit.*   300

---

272 *threat me* threaten me that.   273 *mischiefs* injuries. The word is much
stronger than in modern usage. *return'd again* avenged.   274 *that hath* who
have. Common Elizabethan diction. *hath* Q¹; Q², ᴋ: "have."   276 *heavy* sorrowful.
281 *Lavinia* F²; Q¹: "And, Lauinia."   *things* F¹: Q¹: "Armes."   285 *Hie* hasten.
291 *leaves* ROWE; QQ, F¹: "loues."   293 *tofore* formerly.   294 *now nor* now neither.
296 *requite* revenge.   298 *Tarquin* Tarquinius Superbus, who was banished from
Rome with his queen because his son, Tarquin, had raped Lucrece.   299 *a pow'r*
an army.

◇◇◇◇◇◇◇◇◇◇◇◇◇◇◇◇

[SCENE II. *A room in the house of* Titus.]

A banquet. Enter [Titus] Andronicus, Marcus, Lavinia,
   and the Boy [Lucius].

TIT.   So, so, now sit; and look you eat no more
         Than will preserve just so much strength in us
         As will revenge these bitter woes of ours.
         Marcus, unknit that sorrow-wreathen knot.
         Thy niece and I (poor creatures) want our hands   5
         And cannot passionate our tenfold grief
         With folded arms. This poor right hand of mine
         Is left to tyrannize upon my breast;
         Who, when my heart, all mad with misery,
         Beats in this hollow prison of my flesh,   10
         Then thus I thump it down.
         [*To* Lavinia] Thou map of woe, that thus dost talk in
             signs!
         When thy poor heart beats with outrageous beating,
         Thou canst not strike it thus to make it still.
         Wound it with sighing, girl, kill it with groans;   15
         Or get some little knife between thy teeth
         And just against thy heart make thou a hole,
         That all the tears that thy poor eyes let fall
         May run into that sink, and soaking in,
         Drown the lamenting fool in sea-salt tears.   20

MARC.   Fie, brother, fie! Teach her not thus to lay

III.II. This scene is omitted in the quartos but included in F¹.   1 *look* see that.
4 *unknit . . . knot* unfold your arms. To fold the arms was a sign of sorrow or
melancholy.   5 *want* lack.   6 *passionate* give sufficient signs of passion to express.
12 *map of woe* picture or symbol of sorrow.   15 *Wound it with sighing* It was
believed that every sigh drained a drop of blood from the heart.   19 *sink* receptacle.   20 *fool* poor pitiful creature. The word was commonly used as one of
endearment.

Such violent hands upon her tender life.

TIT.   How now? Has sorrow made thee dote already?
Why, Marcus, no man should be mad but I.
What violent hands can she lay on her life?   25
Ah, wherefore dost thou urge the name of hands,
To bid Æneas tell the tale twice o'er
How Troy was burnt and he made miserable?
O, handle not the theme, to talk of hands,
Lest we remember still that we have none.   30
Fie, fie, how franticly I square my talk,
As if we should forget we had no hands
If Marcus did not name the word of hands!
Come, let's fall to; and, gentle girl, eat this.
Here is no drink! Hark, Marcus, what she says.   35
I can interpret all her martyr'd signs.
She says she drinks no other drink but tears,
Brew'd with her sorrow, mesh'd upon her cheeks.
Speechless complainer, I will learn thy thought.
In thy dumb action will I be as perfect   40
As begging hermits in their holy prayers.
Thou shalt not sigh, nor hold thy stumps to heaven,
Nor wink, nor nod, nor kneel, nor make a sign,
But I (of these) will wrest an alphabet
And by still practice learn to know thy meaning.   45

BOY.   Good grandsire, leave these bitter deep laments.
Make my aunt merry with some pleasing tale.

MARC.   Alas, the tender boy, in passion mov'd,
Doth weep to see his grandsire's heaviness!

TIT.   Peace, tender sapling! Thou art made of tears,   50
And tears will quickly melt thy life away.

---

23 *dote* act foolishly.   26 *urge* put forward.   27–8 *Æneas . . . was burnt* In the
second book of Virgil's ÆNEID Æneas, at the request of Queen Dido, tells the story
of the destruction of Troy.   29 *handle not* do not dwell upon.   30 *still* continually.   31 *square* regulate.   34 *fall to* begin eating.   36 *martyr'd signs* signs
of the mutilated one.   38 *with* by.   *mesh'd* brewed.   40 *perfect* fully under-
standing. To be "perfect" in something is to know it by heart.   43 *wink* close

Marcus strikes the dish with a knife.

What dost thou strike at, Marcus, with thy knife?

MARC. At that that I have kill'd, my lord — a fly.

TIT.   Out on thee, murderer! Thou kill'st my heart.
       Mine eyes are cloy'd with view of tyranny.   55
       A deed of death done on the innocent
       Becomes not Titus' brother. Get thee gone!
       I see thou art not for my company.

MARC. Alas, my lord, I have but kill'd a fly.

TIT.   But? How if that fly had a father and mother?   60
       How would he hang his slender gilded wings
       And buzz lamenting doings in the air!
       Poor harmless fly,
       That, with his pretty buzzing melody,
       Came here to make us merry — and thou hast kill'd him.   65

MARC. Pardon me, sir. It was a black ill-favour'd fly,
       Like to the Empress' Moor. Therefore I kill'd him.

TIT.   O, O, O!
       Then pardon me for reprehending thee,
       For thou hast done a charitable deed.   70
       Give me thy knife, I will insult on him,
       Flattering myself, as if it were the Moor
       Come hither purposely to poison me.
       There's for thyself! and that's for Tamora!
       Ah, sirrah!   75
       Yet, I think, we are not brought so low
       But that between us we can kill a fly
       That comes in likeness of a coal-black Moor.

MARC. Alas, poor man! Grief has so wrought on him

---

the eyes.   **45** *still* constant.   **48** *tender* young.   *passion* sorrow.   **49** *heaviness* sadness.   **62** *lamenting doings* lamentations.   **66** *ill-favour'd* ugly.   **69** *reprehending* rebuking.   **71** *insult on* triumph over.   **72** *Flattering myself* pleasing myself with false belief.   **75** *sirrah* term of address used with servants and other inferiors.

He takes false shadows for true substances.   80

TIT.   Come, take away. Lavinia, go with me.
        I'll to thy closet and go read with thee
        Sad stories chanced in the times of old.
        Come, boy, and go with me. Thy sight is young,
        And thou shalt read when mine begin to dazzle.   *Exeunt.*   85

which Lear foreshadowing

---

80 *shadows* appearances.   81 *take away* clear the table.   82 *closet* private room.
83 *chanced* which took place.   85 *mine* my eyes.   *dazzle* grow dim.

Act Four

◇◇

[SCENE 1. *Rome.* Titus' *garden.*]

Enter Lucius' Son *and* Lavinia *running after him, and
the* Boy *flies from her with his books under his arm.
Enter* Titus *and* Marcus.

BOY. Help, grandsire, help! My aunt Lavinia
Follows me everywhere, I know not why.
Good uncle Marcus, see how swift she comes!
Alas, sweet aunt, I know not what you mean.

MARC. Stand by me, Lucius. Do not fear thine aunt.   5

TIT. She loves thee, boy, too well to do thee harm.

BOY. Ay, when my father was in Rome she did.

MARC. What means my niece Lavinia by these signs?

TIT. Fear her not, Lucius. Somewhat doth she mean.
See, Lucius, see, how much she makes of thee!   10
Somewhither would she have thee go with her.
Ah, boy, Cornelia never with more care
Read to her sons than she hath read to thee
Sweet poetry and Tully's Orator.

IV.I. 9 *Somewhat* something.   11 *Somewhither* someplace. The word does not
occur elsewhere in Shakespeare.   12 *Cornelia* a Roman matron famous for her
careful education of her sons, two political leaders known as the Gracchi.   14
Tully's Orator the DE ORATORE of Cicero.

| MARC. | Canst thou not guess wherefore she plies thee thus? | 15 |

BOY. My lord, I know not, I, nor can I guess,
Unless some fit or frenzy do possess her;
For I have heard my grandsire say full oft,
Extremity of griefs would make men mad;
And I have read that Hecuba of Troy   20
Ran mad for sorrow. That made me to fear;
Although, my lord, I know my noble aunt
Loves me as dear as e'er my mother did,
And would not, but in fury, fright my youth;
Which made me down to throw my books, and fly — 25
Causeless, perhaps. But pardon me, sweet aunt;
And, madam, if my uncle Marcus go,
I will most willingly attend your ladyship.

MARC. Lucius, I will.

> [Lavinia *turns over with her stumps
> the books which* Lucius *has let fall.*]

TIT. How now, Lavinia? Marcus, what means this? 30
Some book there is that she desires to see. —
Which is it, girl, of these? — Open them, boy. —
But thou art deeper read and better skill'd.
Come and take choice of all my library,
And so beguile thy sorrow, till the heavens   35
Reveal the damn'd contriver of this deed.
Why lifts she up her arms in sequence thus?

MARC. I think she means that there were more than one
Confederate in the fact. Ay, more there was;
Or else to heaven she heaves them for revenge. 40

TIT. Lucius, what book is that she tosseth so?

BOY. Grandsire, 'tis Ovid's Metamorphoses.

---

15 *Canst . . . thus* CAPELL; QQ, F¹ add this line to Titus' preceding speech. *plies*
pursues, worries. 20 *Hecuba* wife of Priam, King of Troy. 24 *but in fury*
except in madness. 26 *Causeless* without reason. 28 *attend* wait on. 33 *deeper
. . . skill'd* i.e. than to wish to read the books of a schoolboy. 35 *beguile* find
comfort for. 37 *in sequence* one after the other. 39 *Confederate in the fact*

My mother gave it me.

MARC.   For love of her that's gone
Perhaps she cull'd it from among the rest.

TIT.   Soft! So busily she turns the leaves!   45
Help her! What would she find? Lavinia, shall I read?
This is the tragic tale of Philomel
And treats of Tereus' treason and his rape;
And rape, I fear, was root of thine annoy.

MARC.   See, brother, see! Note how she quotes the leaves.   50

TIT.   Lavinia, wert thou thus surpris'd, sweet girl,
Ravish'd and wrong'd as Philomela was,
Forc'd in the ruthless, vast, and gloomy woods?
See, see!
Ay, such a place there is where we did hunt   55
(O had we never, never hunted there!)
Pattern'd by that the poet here describes,
By nature made for murders and for rapes.

MARC.   O, why should nature build so foul a den,
Unless the gods delight in tragedies?   60

TIT.   Give signs, sweet girl, for here are none but friends,
What Roman lord it was durst do the deed.
Or slunk not Saturnine, as Tarquin erst,
That left the camp to sin in Lucrece' bed?

MARC.   Sit down, sweet niece. Brother, sit down by me.   65
Apollo, Pallas, Jove, or Mercury,
Inspire me, that I may this treason find.
My lord, look here! Look here, Lavinia!

*He writes his name with his staff, and
guides it with feet and mouth.*

This sandy plot is plain. Guide, if thou canst,

---

joined together in the crime.   41 *tosseth* turns the leaves of.   49 *thine* F[1]; Q[1]:
"thy." *annoy* injury.   50 *quotes* marks (Q[2]; Q[1]: "coats").   51 *surpris'd* suddenly
attacked.   53 *Forc'd* raped. *ruthless* pitiless. *vast* desolate.   57 *Pattern'd by
that* similar in appearance or shape to what.   63 *slunk* crept stealthily. *erst*
once.   64 *That* who.   69 *plain* flat.

This after me. I have writ my name   70
Without the help of any hand at all.
Curs'd be that heart that forc'd us to this shift!
Write thou, good niece, and here display at last
What God will have discovered for revenge.
Heaven guide thy pen to print thy sorrows plain,   75
That we may know the traitors and the truth!

> *She takes the staff in her mouth and*
> *guides it with her stumps and writes.*

TIT.   O, do ye read, my lord, what she hath writ?
         "Stuprum — Chiron — Demetrius."

MARC.   What, what? the lustful sons of Tamora
         Performers of this heinous bloody deed?   80

TIT.   *Magni dominator poli,*
         Tam lentus audis scelera? tam lentus vides?

MARC.   O, calm thee, gentle lord! although I know
         There is enough written upon this earth
         To stir a mutiny in the mildest thoughts   85
         And arm the minds of infants to exclaims.
         My lord, kneel down with me; Lavinia, kneel;
         And kneel, sweet boy, the Roman Hector's hope;
         And swear with me — as with the woeful feere
         And father of that chaste dishonoured dame   90
         Lord Junius Brutus sware for Lucrece' rape —
         That we will prosecute by good advice
         Mortal revenge upon these traitorous Goths,
         And see their blood or die with this reproach.

---

70 *This after me* do as I have done.   72 *shift* necessary device.   74 *discovered
for revenge* revealed so that it may be avenged.   78 *Stuprum* rape.   81–2 *Magni
. . . vides* great ruler of the heavens, are you so slow to hear crimes, so slow to
see them? From the PHÆDRA of Seneca, lines 671–2.   85 *stir* arouse.   86 *exclaims*
cries of protest.   88 *the Roman . . . hope* the hope for the future of Titus
Andronicus, who is the champion of Rome as Hector was the champion of Troy.
The Romans considered themselves to be descended from the Trojans.   89 *feere*
husband.   91 *Junius Brutus* He led the rebellion which drove the Tarquins out
of Rome following the rape of Lucrece. He was reputedly the ancestor of the
Brutus of Shakespeare's JULIUS CÆSAR. *sware* swore.   92 *by good advice* after

TIT.	'Tis sure enough, an you knew how.	95
	But if you hunt these bear-whelps, then beware.	
	The dam will wake; and if she wind ye once,	
	She's with the lion deeply still in league,	
	And lulls him whilst she playeth on her back,	
	And when he sleeps will she do what she list.	100
	You are a young huntsman, Marcus; let't alone;	
	And come, I will go get a leaf of brass,	
	And with a gad of steel will write these words,	
	And lay it by. The angry northen wind	
	Will blow these sands like Sibyl's leaves abroad,	105
	And where's our lesson then? Boy, what say you?	
BOY.	I say, my lord, that if I were a man,	
	Their mother's bedchamber should not be safe	
	For these base bondmen to the yoke of Rome.	
MARC.	Ay, that's my boy! Thy father hath full oft	110
	For his ungrateful country done the like.	
BOY.	And, uncle, so will I, an if I live.	
TIT.	Come go with me into mine armory.	
	Lucius, I'll fit thee; and withal my boy	
	Shall carry from me to the Empress' sons	115
	Presents that I intend to send them both.	
	Come, come! Thou'lt do my message, wilt thou not?	
BOY.	Ay, with my dagger in their bosoms, grandsire.	
TIT.	No, boy, not so. I'll teach thee another course.	
	Lavinia, come. Marcus, look to my house.	120
	Lucius and I'll go brave it at the court.	

careful planning.   94 *with this reproach* i.e. with the stigma of not having achieved revenge.   97 *dam* mother bear. *wind ye* smell your scent.   98 *still* always.   100 *list* pleases.   102 *leaf* sheet (for engraving).   103 *gad* sharp point.   104 *northen* northern (a common dialectal form).   105 *these sands* i.e. what Lavinia has written in the sand. *Sibyl's leaves* The prophecies of the Sibyl of Cumae were delivered by leaves which she placed upon the ground and which were later blown away by the wind.   109 *bondmen . . . Rome* slaves of the Romans (which the sons of Tamora still were).   114 *fit thee* provide you with armour. *withal* at the same time.   121 *brave it* swagger defiantly.

> Ay, marry, will we, sir! and we'll be waited on.

>> *Exeunt* [Titus, Lavinia, *and* Young
>> Lucius].

MARC.   O heavens, can you hear a good man groan
   And not relent, or not compassion him?
   Marcus, attend him in his ecstasy,   125
   That hath more scars of sorrow in his heart
   Than foemen's marks upon his batt'red shield,
   But yet so just that he will not revenge.
   Revenge the heavens for old Andronicus!   *Exit.*

◇◇◇◇◇◇◇◇◇◇◇◇◇◇◇◇

[SCENE II. *Rome. The Palace.*]

Enter Aaron, Chiron, *and* Demetrius *at one door; and
 at the other door* Young Lucius *and another, with a
 bundle of weapons, and verses writ upon them.*

CHI. Demetrius, here's the son of Lucius.
   He hath some message to deliver us.

AAR. Ay, some mad message from his mad grandfather.

BOY. My lords, with all the humbleness I may,
   I greet your Honours from Andronicus —   5
   [*Aside*] And pray the Roman gods confound you both!

DEM. Gramercy, lovely Lucius. What's the news?

BOY. [*aside*] That you are both decipher'd, that's the news,
   For villains mark'd with rape. — May it please you,

---

122 *waited on* listened to (and not ignored as we have been in the past). 124
compassion pity. 125 *ecstasy* madness. 129 *Revenge the heavens* let the heavens
avenge.

 IV.II. 6 *confound* destroy. 7 *Gramercy* thanks. 8 *decipher'd* unmasked, revealed. 10 *well advis'd* after careful consideration. 11 *goodliest* finest. 16
appointed equipped. 20-1 *Integer vitae . . . nec arcu* the man of upright life
and free from crime need not fear the Moorish javelins or bows. These are the

My grandsire, well advis'd, hath sent by me   10
The goodliest weapons of his armory
To gratify your honourable youth,
The hope of Rome; for so he bid me say;
And so I do, and with his gifts present
Your lordships, that, whenever you have need,   15
You may be armed and appointed well.
And so I leave you both — [*aside*] like bloody villains.

                              Exit [*with* Attendant].

DEM.   What's here? A scroll, and written round about?
         Let's see.

         [*Reads*] *Integer vitae scelerisque purus*   20
                   Non eget Mauri iaculis nec arcu.

CHI.   O, 'tis a verse in Horace. I know it well.
         I read it in the grammar long ago.

AAR.   Ay, just — a verse in Horace. Right, you have it!
         [*Aside*] Now what a thing it is to be an ass!   25
         Here's no sound jest! The old man hath found their guilt,
         And sends them weapons wrapp'd about with lines
         That wound (beyond their feeling) to the quick.
         But were our witty Empress well afoot,
         She would applaud Andronicus' conceit.   30
         But let her rest in her unrest awhile. —
         And now, young lords, was't not a happy star
         Led us to Rome, strangers, and more than so,
         Captives, to be advanced to this height?
         It did me good, before the palace gate   35
         To brave the Tribune in his brother's hearing.

DEM.   But me more good to see so great a lord

---

opening lines of Horace, ODES, I.XXII, one of the best known of all classical poems.
23 *the grammar* William Lyly's LATIN GRAMMAR, widely used by Elizabethan schoolboys, where this quotation from Horace twice appears.   24 *just* exactly.   26
sound wholesome. *found* discovered.   28 *their feeling* their ability to compre-
hend.   29 *witty* quick-witted, ingenious. *well afoot* up and about.   30 *conceit*
device, clever trick.   31 *rest in her unrest* remain in her inactive condition (in
childbed).   36 *brave* insult and defy.

    Basely insinuate, and send us gifts.

AAR.   Had he not reason, Lord Demetrius?
    Did you not use his daughter very friendly?   40

DEM.   I would we had a thousand Roman dames
    At such a bay, by turn to serve our lust.

CHI.   A charitable wish and full of love!

AAR.   Here lacks but your mother for to say amen.

CHI.   And that would she for twenty thousand more.   45

DEM.   Come, let us go and pray to all the gods
    For our beloved mother in her pains.

AAR.   [aside] Pray to the devils. The gods have given us over.

                            Trumpets sound.

DEM.   Why do the Emperor's trumpets flourish thus?

CHI.   Belike for joy the Emperor hath a son.   50

DEM.   Soft! Who comes here?

              Enter Nurse, *with a blackamoor* Child.

NURSE.   Good morrow, lords.
    O, tell me, did you see Aaron the Moor?

AAR.   Well, more or less, or ne'er a whit at all!
    Here Aaron is; and what with Aaron now?

NURSE.   O gentle Aaron, we are all undone!   55
    Now help, or woe betide thee evermore!

AAR.   Why, what a caterwauling dost thou keep!
    What dost thou wrap and fumble in thine arms?

NURSE.   O, that which I would hide from heaven's eye —

38 *insinuate* curry favour.   42 *At such a bay* trapped in such a fashion (an expression from hunting).   45 *more* Roman dames to be ravished.   47 *pains* labours of childbirth.   48 *given us over* abandoned us.   50 *Belike* probably.   53 *more or less* He puts on "Moor." *ne'er a whit* never a bit.   55 *gentle* noble. *undone* ruined.   56 *woe betide* misfortune befall.   58 *thine* Q²; Q¹: "thy."   61 *is delivered* has given birth.   64 *dam* mother.   65 *issue* birth.   68 *fair-fac'd* light-

	Our Empress' shame and stately Rome's disgrace! 60
	She is delivered, lords; she is delivered.
AAR.	To whom?
NURSE.	I mean she is brought abed.
AAR.	Well, God give her good rest! What hath he sent her?
NURSE.	A devil.
AAR.	Why, then she is the devil's dam —
	A joyful issue! 65
NURSE.	A joyless, dismal, black, and sorrowful issue!
	Here is the babe, as loathsome as a toad
	Amongst the fair-fac'd breeders of our clime.
	The Empress sends it thee, thy stamp, thy seal,
	And bids thee christen it with thy dagger's point. 70
AAR.	Zounds, ye whore! is black so base a hue?
	Sweet blowse, you are a beauteous blossom sure.
DEM.	Villain, what hast thou done?
AAR.	That which thou canst not undo.
CHI.	Thou hast undone our mother. 75
AAR.	Villain, I have done thy mother.
DEM.	And therein, hellish dog, thou hast undone her.
	Woe to her chance, and damn'd her loathed choice!
	Accurs'd the offspring of so foul a fiend!
CHI.	It shall not live. 80
AAR.	It shall not die.
NURSE.	Aaron, it must. The mother wills it so.
AAR.	What, must it, nurse? Then let no man but I
	Do execution on my flesh and blood.

i don't like this

---

complexioned (Q¹; Q³, K: "fairest"). *breeders* A term used with animals. *clime*
country. 69 *thy stamp, thy seal* what you have created and confirmed as yours.
71 *Zounds* by God's wounds. 72 *blowse* ruddy-cheeked little girl. In applying the
term to his black child Aaron is being ironic. 75 *undone* (a) ruined (b) un-
dressed. 76 *done* had sexual relations with. 78 *chance* luck.

DEM.   I'll broach the tadpole on my rapier's point.   85
        Nurse, give it me! My sword shall soon dispatch it.

AAR.   Sooner this sword shall plough thy bowels up.

                        [*Takes the* Child *from the* Nurse, *and*
                        draws.]

        Stay, murderous villains! Will you kill your brother?
        Now by the burning tapers of the sky,
        That shone so brightly when this boy was got,   90
        He dies upon my scimitar's sharp point
        That touches this my first-born son and heir!
        I tell you, younglings, not Enceladus,
        With all his threat'ning band of Typhon's brood,
        Nor great Alcides, nor the god of war,   95
        Shall seize this prey out of his father's hands.
        What, what, ye sanguine, shallow-hearted boys!
        Ye white-lim'd walls! ye alehouse painted signs!
        Coal-black is better than another hue
        In that it scorns to bear another hue;   100
        For all the water in the ocean
        Can never turn the swan's black legs to white,
        Although she lave them hourly in the flood.
        Tell the Empress from me I am of age
        To keep mine own — excuse it how she can.   105

DEM.   Wilt thou betray thy noble mistress thus?

AAR.   My mistress is my mistress; this myself,
        The vigour and the picture of my youth.
        This before all the world do I prefer;
        This maugre all the world will I keep safe,   110

85 *broach* spit, as on the point of a sword.   86 *dispatch it* finish it off.   89
burning tapers i.e. stars.   90 *got* begotten, conceived.   93 *younglings* boys (a
contemptuous expression). *Enceladus* one of the Titans, the sons of Typhon, who
waged war on the gods of Greek mythology.   94 *brood* offspring.   95 *Alcides*
Hercules. *god of war* Mars.   97 *sanguine* pink-cheeked. *shallow-hearted* cowardly.
98 *white-lim'd walls* i.e. hypocrites. Whitewashed exteriors may hide the blackness
within. There may be an allusion to MATTHEW, XXIII, 27. *alehouse . . . signs* crudely
painted imitations of men (like the portraits on the signs of alehouses).   99 *another hue* any other colour.   103 *lave* wash.   104 *of age* sufficiently mature.   107
this this child.   110 *maugre* in spite of.   111 *smoke* suffer. The metaphor is

Or some of you shall smoke for it in Rome!

DEM.   By this our mother is for ever sham'd.

CHI.   Rome will despise her for this foul escape.

NURSE. The Emperor in his rage will doom her death.

CHI.   I blush to think upon this ignomy.   115

AAR.   Why, there's the privilege your beauty bears.
        Fie, treacherous hue, that will betray with blushing
        The close enacts and counsels of thy heart!
        Here's a young lad fram'd of another leer.
        Look how the black slave smiles upon the father,   120
        As who should say "Old lad, I am thine own."
        He is your brother, lords, sensibly fed
        Of that self blood that first gave life to you;
        And from that womb where you imprisoned were
        He is enfranchised and come to light.   125
        Nay, he is your brother by the surer side,
        Although my seal be stamped in his face.

NURSE. Aaron, what shall I say unto the Empress?

DEM.   Advise thee, Aaron, what is to be done,
        And we will all subscribe to thy advice.   130
        Save thou the child, so we may all be safe.

AAR.   Then sit we down and let us all consult.
        My son and I will have the wind of you.
        Keep there. Now talk at pleasure of your safety.

DEM.   How many women saw this child of his?   135

AAR.   Why, so, brave lords! When we join in league,

---

from burning at the stake.   113 *escape* outrageous transgression (specifically
sexual).   114 *doom her death* sentence her to death.   115 *ignomy* ignominy, dis-
grace.   118 *close enacts* secret intentions.   119 *leer* complexion.   121 *As who
should say* like one who is saying.   122 *sensibly* obviously, as is plain to the
senses.   124 *from that* Q³; Q¹: "from your."   125 *is enfranchised* has been liber-
ated.   126 *by the surer side* i.e. through the mother. Maternity can always be
more surely ascertained than paternity.   129 *Advise thee* consider carefully.   130
subscribe . . . advice agree to your decision.   133 *have . . . of you* watch you
carefully (lest you betray us). An expression from hunting: game is watched down
wind by the hunter.   136 *brave* fine.

I am a lamb; but if you brave the Moor,
The chafed boar, the mountain lioness,
The ocean swells not so as Aaron storms.
But say again, how many saw the child?   140

NURSE.   Cornelia the midwife and myself;
And no one else but the delivered Empress.

AAR.   The Empress, the midwife, and yourself —
Two may keep counsel when the third's away.
Go to the Empress; tell her this I said!   *He kills her.* 145
Weeke, weeke! — So cries a pig prepared to the spit.

DEM.   What mean'st thou, Aaron? Wherefore didst thou this?

AAR.   O Lord, sir, 'tis a deed of policy!
Shall she live to betray this guilt of ours —
A long-tongu'd babbling gossip? No, lords, no.   150
And now be it known to you my full intent.
Not far one Muli lives, my countryman,
His wife but yesternight was brought to bed;
His child is like to her, fair as you are.
Go pack with him, and give the mother gold,   155
And tell them both the circumstance of all;
And how by this their child shall be advanc'd,
And be received for the Emperor's heir
And substituted in the place of mine,
To calm this tempest whirling in the court;   160
And let the Emperor dandle him for his own.
Hark ye, lords. You see I have given her physic,
And you must needs bestow her funeral.
The fields are near, and you are gallant grooms.
This done, see that you take no longer days,   165
But send the midwife presently to me.
The midwife and the nurse well made away,

---

137 *brave* insult, defy.   138 *chafed* enraged.   144 *Two may . . . away* A proverbial expression.   148 *policy* trickery for political purposes. The word was especially associated with the Elizabethan "Machiavel."   152 *Muli lives* STEEVENS; Q¹:
"Muliteus."   154 *is like to* resembles. *fair* light-complexioned.   155 *pack* con-
spire, make arrangements.   156 *the circumstance of all* all the particulars.   157
advanc'd raised in rank.   162 *physic* medicine.   163 *bestow* make provisions

           Then let the ladies tattle what they please.

CHI.   Aaron, I see thou wilt not trust the air
           With secrets.

DEM.   For this care of Tamora,   170
           Herself and hers are highly bound to thee.

                     Exeunt [Demetrius *and* Chiron, *bear-
                     ing off the dead* Nurse].

AAR.   Now to the Goths, as swift as swallow flies,
           There to dispose this treasure in mine arms
           And secretly to greet the Empress' friends.
           Come on, you thick-lipp'd slave, I'll bear you hence;   175
           For it is you that puts us to our shifts.
           I'll make you feed on berries and on roots,
           And feed on curds and whey, and suck the goat,
           And cabin in a cave, and bring you up
           To be a warrior and command a camp.   *Exit.*   180

❖❖❖❖❖❖❖❖❖❖❖❖❖❖❖

[SCENE III. *Rome. A public place.*]

      Enter Titus, Old Marcus, Young Lucius, *and other* Gen-
      tlemen, [Publius, Sempronius, *and* Caius,] *with bows,
      and* Titus *bears the arrows with letters on the ends of
      them.*

TIT.   Come, Marcus, come. Kinsmen, this is the way.
           Sir boy, let me see your archery:
           Look ye draw home enough, and 'tis there straight.
           Terras Astraea reliquit,

---

for.   164 *grooms* fellows.   165 *days* time.   166 *presently* immediately.   167 *well
made away* properly disposed of.   171 *hers* her family.   173 *dispose* make use of.
176 *puts . . . shifts* causes us to resort to extreme devices.   179 *cabin* reside.

   IV.III. 3 *Look . . . enough* see that you draw your bow as fully as it can be
drawn.   4 *Terras . . . reliquit* Astraea, goddess of justice, has left the earth. From
Ovid's METAMORPHOSES, I, 150.

Be you rememb'red, Marcus: she's gone, she's fled.   5
Sirs, take you to your tools. You, cousins, shall
Go sound the ocean, and cast your nets;
Happily you may catch her in the sea.
Yet there's as little justice as at land.
No! Publius and Sempronius, you must do it.   10
'Tis you must dig with mattock and with spade
And pierce the inmost centre of the earth;
Then, when you come to Pluto's region,
I pray you deliver him this petition.
Tell him it is for justice and for aid,   15
And that it comes from old Andronicus,
Shaken with sorrows in ungrateful Rome.
Ah, Rome! Well, well, I made thee miserable
What time I threw the people's suffrages
On him that thus doth tyrannize o'er me.   20
Go get you gone; and pray be careful all,
And leave you not a man-of-war unsearch'd.
This wicked emperor may have shipp'd her hence;
And, kinsmen, then we may go pipe for justice.

MARC.   O Publius, is not this a heavy case,   25
        To see thy noble uncle thus distract?

PUB.   Therefore, my lords, it highly us concerns
        By day and night t' attend him carefully,
        And feed his humour kindly as we may
        Till time beget some careful remedy.   30

MARC.   Kinsmen, his sorrows are past remedy.
        Join with the Goths, and with revengeful war
        Take wreak on Rome for this ingratitude,
        And vengeance on the traitor Saturnine.

TIT.   Publius, how now? How now, my masters?   35

---

5 *Be you rememb'red* remember.   7 *sound* probe the depth of.   8 *Happily* perhaps.   13 *Pluto's region* Hades, the underworld, of which Pluto was king.   19 *What time* at the time when.   *suffrages* votes.   24 *go pipe* whistle in vain.   25 *heavy case* sorrowful situation.   26 *distract* out of his mind.   28 *attend* watch over.   29 *feed his humour* cater to his whim.   30 *careful* curing.   33 *wreak* vengeance.   36 *met with her* found Astraea, justice.   39 *for* as for.   41 *perforce* of necessity.   *stay a time* wait a while.   42 *feed me with delays* put me off with

What, have you met with her?

PUB.   No, my good lord; but Pluto sends you word,
       If you will have Revenge from hell, you shall.
       Marry, for Justice, she is so employ'd,
       He thinks, with Jove in heaven, or somewhere else,   40
       So that perforce you must needs stay a time.

TIT.   He doth me wrong to feed me with delays.
       I'll dive into the burning lake below
       And pull her out of Acheron by the heels.
       Marcus, we are but shrubs, no cedars we,   45
       No big-bon'd men fram'd of the Cyclops' size;
       But metal, Marcus, steel to the very back,
       Yet wrung with wrongs more than our backs can bear;
       And, sith there is no justice in earth nor hell,
       We will solicit heaven, and move the gods   50
       To send down Justice for to wreak our wrongs.
       Come, to this gear. You are a good archer, Marcus.

                          He gives them the arrows.

       "Ad Jovem," that's for you. Here, "Ad Apollinem,"
       "Ad Martem," that's for myself.
       Here, boy, "To Pallas." Here, "To Mercury."   55
       "To Saturn," Caius — not to Saturnine!
       You were as good to shoot against the wind.
       To it, boy! Marcus, loose when I bid.
       Of my word, I have written to effect;
       There's not a god left unsolicited.   60

MARC. Kinsmen, shoot all your shafts into the court.
       We will afflict the Emperor in his pride.

TIT.   Now, masters, draw. [*They shoot.*] O, well said, Lucius!

---

false promises.   44 *Acheron* one of the rivers of the classical Hades.   46 *of the
Cyclops' size* as large as the Cyclops, one-eyed giants who worked at the forge of
the god Vulcan.   49 *sith* since.   51 *wreak* avenge.   52 *to this gear* about this
business.   53 *Ad Jovem* to Jove. *Ad Apollinem* to Apollo.   54 *Ad Martem* to
Mars.   55 *Pallas* Pallas Athene or Minerva, goddess of wisdom.   56 *To Saturn,
Caius* CAPELL; QQ, F¹: "To Saturnine, to Caius."   57 *were . . . shoot* would do
as much good as by shooting.   58 *loose* i.e. your arrow.   59 *to effect* effectively.

          Good boy, in Virgo's lap! Give it Pallas.

MARC.   My lord, I aim a mile beyond the moon.   65
          Your letter is with Jupiter by this.

TIT.   Ha, ha!
          Publius, Publius, what hast thou done?
          See, see, thou hast shot off one of Taurus' horns!

MARC.   This was the sport, my lord. When Publius shot,   70
          The Bull, being gall'd, gave Aries such a knock
          That down fell both the Ram's horns in the court;
          And who should find them but the Empress' villain?
          She laugh'd, and told the Moor he should not choose
          But give them to his master for a present.   75

TIT.   Why, there it goes! God give his lordship joy!

                 Enter the Clown, *with a basket, and*
                 two pigeons in it.

          News, news from heaven! Marcus, the post is come.
          Sirrah, what tidings? Have you any letters?
          Shall I have justice? What says Jupiter?

CLOWN.   Who? the gibbet-maker? He says that he hath taken them   80
          down again, for the man must not be hang'd till the
          next week.

TIT.   But what says Jupiter I ask thee?

CLOWN.   Alas, sir, I know not Jupiter. I never drank with him
          in all my life.   85

TIT.   Why, villain, art not thou the carrier?

CLOWN.   Ay, of my pigeons, sir; nothing else.

TIT.   Why, didst thou not come from heaven?

CLOWN.   From heaven? Alas, sir, I never came there. God forbid

---

64 *Virgo* the virgin, a constellation.   69 *Taurus* the bull, one of the signs of the
zodiac.   71 *gall'd* irritated. *Aries* the ram, another sign of the zodiac.   73 *villain*
servant.   75 *But give . . . present* The proverbial joke about the horns of the
cuckold.   76 *there it goes* a hunter's cry of encouragement.   77 *News* Q¹ precedes
this with the speech prefix, "Clowne."   80 *Who* ROWE; Q¹: "Ha." *gibbet-maker*
The Clown takes "Jupiter" as "gibbeter." *them* the gallows or the gibbet.   86

I should be so bold to press to heaven in my young days. 90
Why, I am going with my pigeons to the Tribunal
Plebs, to take up a matter of brawl betwixt my uncle
and one of the emperal's men.

MARC.   Why, sir, that is as fit as can be to serve for your oration; and let him deliver the pigeons to the Emperor   95
from you.

TIT.   Tell me, can you deliver an oration to the Emperor
with a grace?

CLOWN.   Nay, truly, sir, I could never say grace in all my life.

TIT.   Sirrah, come hither. Make no more ado,   100
But give your pigeons to the Emperor.
By me thou shalt have justice at his hands.
Hold, hold! Meanwhile here's money for thy charges.
Give me pen and ink. Sirrah, can you with a grace
deliver up a supplication?   105

CLOWN.   Ay, sir.

TIT.   Then here is a supplication for you. And when you
come to him, at the first approach you must kneel; then
kiss his foot; then deliver up your pigeons; and then
look for your reward. I'll be at hand, sir. See you do it 110
bravely.

CLOWN.   I warrant you, sir. Let me alone.

TIT.   Sirrah, hast thou a knife? Come, let me see it.
Here, Marcus, fold it in the oration;
For thou hast made it like an humble suppliant.   115
And when thou hast given it to the Emperor,
Knock at my door and tell me what he says.

CLOWN.   God be with you, sir; I will.   *Exit.*

TIT.   Come, Marcus, let us go. Publius, follow me.   *Exeunt.*

---

carrier the Elizabethan equivalent of our postman.   90 *press to* push eagerly
towards.   91–2 *Tribunal Plebs* the "tribunus plebis" — one of ten officials who
heard the legal complaints of the common people.   93 *emperal's* emperor's (Q¹;
Q², K: "Emperialls").   98 *with a grace* gracefully.   103 *Hold* here you are.
charges expenses (the cost of the pigeons).   105 *up* Q¹; not in Q², K. *supplication*
petition.   111 *bravely* finely, properly.   112 *Let me alone* leave it to me.

◇◇◇◇◇◇◇◇◇◇◇◇◇◇◇◇◇

[SCENE IV. *Rome. Before the Palace.*]

Enter Emperor *and* Empress, *and her two* Sons, [De-
metrius *and* Chiron; Lords, *and others*]. *The* Emperor *brings the arrows in his hand that* Titus *shot
at him.*

SAT. Why, lords, what wrongs are these! Was ever seen
  An emperor in Rome thus overborne,
  Troubled, confronted thus; and, for the extent
  Of egal justice, us'd in such contempt?
  My lords, you know, as know the mightful gods,   5
  However these disturbers of our peace
  Buzz in the people's ears, there naught hath pass'd,
  But even with law, against the wilful sons
  Of old Andronicus. And what an if
  His sorrows have so overwhelm'd his wits?   10
  Shall we be thus afflicted in his wreaks,
  His fits, his frenzy, and his bitterness?
  And now he writes to heaven for his redress.
  See, here's *To Jove,* and this *To Mercury;*
  This *To Apollo;* this *To the god of war.*   15
  Sweet scrolls to fly about the streets of Rome!
  What's this but libelling against the Senate
  And blazoning our unjustice everywhere?
  A goodly humour, is it not, my lords?
  As who would say, in Rome no justice were.   20
  But if I live, his feigned ecstasies
  Shall be no shelter to these outrages;
  But he and his shall know that justice lives

IV.IV. 2 *overborne* defied, dominated. 3 *the extent* extending, the exercise. 4
egal equal. *us'd in* treated with. 5 *know, as know the* GLOBE; Q¹: "know the."
mightful mighty. 6 *However* no matter what. 7 *Buzz* whisper. 7–8 *there
naught . . . with law* nothing has been done which was not in strict conformity
with justice. 8 *wilful* obstinate. 9 *an if* if. 11 *in his wreaks* by his acts of
vengeance. 18 *blazoning* advertising, publicly proclaiming. *unjustice* injustice.
19 *humour* whim, caprice. 21 *feigned ecstasies* pretended fits of madness. 23

In Saturninus' health; whom, if she sleep,
He'll so awake as she in fury shall   25
Cut off the proud'st conspirator that lives.

TAM.   My gracious lord, my lovely Saturnine,
Lord of my life, commander of my thoughts,
Calm thee, and bear the faults of Titus' age,
Th' effects of sorrow for his valiant sons,   30
Whose loss hath pierc'd him deep and scarr'd his heart;
And rather comfort his distressed plight
Than prosecute the meanest or the best
For these contempts. (*Aside*) Why, thus it shall become
High-witted Tamora to gloze with all.   35
But, Titus, I have touch'd thee to the quick,
Thy lifeblood out. If Aaron now be wise,
Then is all safe, the anchor in the port.

Enter Clown.

How now, good fellow? Wouldst thou speak with us?

CLOWN. Yea, forsooth, an your mistriship be Emperial.   40

TAM.   Empress I am, but yonder sits the Emperor.

CLOWN. 'Tis he. — God and Saint Stephen give you god-den. I
have brought you a letter and a couple of pigeons here.

[Saturninus] *reads the letter.*

SAT.   Go take him away, and hang him presently.

CLOWN. How much money must I have?   45

TAM.   Come, sirrah, you must be hang'd.

CLOWN. Hang'd? By'r Lady, then I have brought up a neck to a
fair end.   *Exit* [*guarded*].

---

and his and his family.   24 *in Saturninus' health* so long as Saturninus is healthy.
she justice (ROWE; QQ, F¹, K: "he").   25 *she* ROWE; QQ, F¹, K: "he."   33 *meanest or
the best* lowest or highest in social position.   34 *contempts* insults.   35 *gloze*
use flattering, pleasant language.   36 *touch'd . . . quick* mortally wounded you.
37 *Thy lifeblood out* once your lifeblood is spilled.   42 *god-den* good evening.
44 *presently* at once.   47 *By'r Lady* K; Q¹: "be Lady"; F¹: "ber Lady."

SAT.   Despiteful and intolerable wrongs!
        Shall I endure this monstrous villainy?   50
        I know from whence this same device proceeds.
        May this be borne? As if his traitorous sons,
        That died by law for murder of our brother,
        Have by my means been butchered wrongfully!
        Go drag the villain hither by the hair!   55
        Nor age nor honour shall shape privilege.
        For this proud mock I'll be thy slaughterman,
        Sly frantic wretch, that holp'st to make me great
        In hope thyself should govern Rome and me!

Enter Nuntius Æmilius.

        What news with thee, Æmilius?   60

ÆMIL.   Arm, my lords! Rome never had more cause!
        The Goths have gathered head; and with a power
        Of high-resolved men, bent to the spoil,
        They hither march amain, under conduct
        Of Lucius, son to old Andronicus;   65
        Who threats in course of this revenge to do
        As much as ever Coriolanus did.

SAT.   Is warlike Lucius general of the Goths?
        These tidings nip me; and I hang the head
        As flowers with frost or grass beat down with storms.   70
        Ay, now begins our sorrows to approach.
        'Tis he the common people love so much;
        Myself hath often overheard them say,
        When I have walked like a private man,
        That Lucius' banishment was wrongfully,   75
        And they have wish'd that Lucius were their emperor.

---

49 *Despiteful* spiteful, malicious.   56 *Nor age* neither age. *shape privilege* provide immunity from the law.   57 *slaughterman* executioner.   58 *holp'st* did help. 59 *s.d. Nuntius* messenger.   62 *gathered head* raised an army. *power* force.   63 *high-resolved* resolutely determined. *bent to the spoil* intent upon plunder.   64 *amain* swiftly. *conduct* the command.   66 *threats* threatens.   67 *Coriolanus* an early Roman hero who led an army of Volscians against his native city. He is the subject of Shakespeare's final tragedy.   69 *nip me* pinch me with cold (like flowers

TAM.   Why should you fear? Is not your city strong?

SAT.   Ay, but the citizens favour Lucius
         And will revolt from me to succour him.

TAM.   King, be thy thoughts imperious like thy name.   80
         Is the sun dimm'd that gnats do fly in it?
         The eagle suffers little birds to sing,
         And is not careful what they mean thereby,
         Knowing that with the shadow of his wings
         He can at pleasure stint their melody.   85
         Even so mayest thou the giddy men of Rome.
         Then cheer thy spirit; for know thou, Emperor,
         I will enchant the old Andronicus
         With words more sweet, and yet more dangerous,
         Than baits to fish or honey stalks to sheep,   90
         When as the one is wounded with the bait,
         The other rotted with delicious feed.

SAT.   But he will not entreat his son for us.

TAM.   If Tamora entreat him, then he will;
         For I can smooth, and fill his aged ears   95
         With golden promises, that, were his heart
         Almost impregnable, his old ears deaf,
         Yet should both ear and heart obey my tongue.
         [*To Æmilius*] Go thou before to be our ambassador;
         Say that the Emperor requests a parley   100
         Of warlike Lucius, and appoint the meeting
         Even at his father's house, the old Andronicus.

SAT.   Æmilius, do this message honourably;
         And if he stand on hostage for his safety,

---

attacked by frost).   74 *walked like* gone about disguised as.   77 *strong* well
fortified.   79 *succour* help.   81 *that* because.   82 *suffers* permits.   83 *careful*
troubled by.   85 *stint* stop.   86 *giddy men* the populace, conventionally regarded
in the Renaissance as irrational and easily moved.   90 *honey stalks* clover, a
surfeit of which was believed to cause illness in sheep.   93 *entreat* plead with.
95 *smooth* flatter.   97 *old ears* F¹; Q¹: "old yeares."   99 *before* ahead.   104
stand on insist upon.   *on* F⁴; QQ, F¹: "in."

| | Bid him demand what pledge will please him best. | 105 |

ÆMIL.   Your bidding shall I do effectually.   *Exit.*

TAM.   Now will I to that old Andronicus
         And temper him with all the art I have
         To pluck proud Lucius from the warlike Goths.
         And now, sweet Emperor, be blithe again   110
         And bury all thy fear in my devices.

SAT.   Then go successantly, and plead to him.   *Exeunt.*

---

105 *demand what* request whatever.   108 *temper* work on.   111 *devices* schemes.
112 *successantly* with success. CAPELL, followed by some editors, reads "incessantly."

Act Five

◇◇◇

[SCENE I. *Plains near Rome.*]

Flourish. Enter Lucius, *with an army of* Goths, *with*
Drum *and* Soldiers.

LUC.   Approved warriors and my faithful friends,
I have received letters from great Rome
Which signifies what hate they bear their Emperor
And how desirous of our sight they are.
Therefore, great lords, be as your titles witness,   5
Imperious, and impatient of your wrongs;
And wherein Rome hath done you any scath,
Let him make treble satisfaction.

GOTH.   Brave slip sprung from the great Andronicus,
Whose name was once our terror, now our comfort,   10
Whose high exploits and honourable deeds
Ingrateful Rome requites with foul contempt,
Be bold in us. We'll follow where thou lead'st,
Like stinging bees in hottest summer's day,
Led by their master to the flow'red fields,   15
And be aveng'd on cursed Tamora.

V.I. 1 *Approved warriors* soldiers tested by battle.   2 *letters* a letter (from the
Latin "litterae").   5 *witness* give evidence.   6 *impatient of* unwilling to endure.
7 *scath* injury.   8 *him* Saturnine.   9 *slip* offshoot.   12 *requites* repays.   13 *Be
bold* have confidence.   15 *their master* What we today call the "queen bee" in
Shakespeare's day was called the "king."

79

OMNES.   And as he saith, so say we all with him.

LUC.   I humbly thank him, and I thank you all.
             But who comes here, led by a lusty Goth?

                         Enter a Goth, *leading of* Aaron *with*
                         his Child *in his arms.*

GOTH.   Renowmed Lucius, from our troops I stray'd   20
             To gaze upon a ruinous monastery;
             And as I earnestly did fix mine eye
             Upon the wasted building, suddenly
             I heard a child cry underneath a wall.
             I made unto the noise, when soon I heard   25
             The crying babe controll'd with this discourse:
             "Peace, tawny slave, half me and half thy dam!
             Did not thy hue bewray whose brat thou art,
             Had nature lent thee but thy mother's look,
             Villain, thou mightst have been an emperor.   30
             But where the bull and cow are both milk-white,
             They never do beget a coal-black calf.
             Peace, villain, peace!" — even thus he rates the babe —
             "For I must bear thee to a trusty Goth,
             Who, when he knows thou art the Empress' babe,   35
             Will hold thee dearly for thy mother's sake."
             With this, my weapon drawn, I rush'd upon him,
             Surpris'd him suddenly, and brought him hither
             To use as you think needful of the man.

LUC.   O worthy Goth, this is the incarnate devil   40
             That robb'd Andronicus of his good hand.
             This is the pearl that pleas'd your Empress' eye;
             And here's the base fruit of her burning lust.
             Say, wall-ey'd slave, whither wouldst thou convey

---

19 *lusty* vigorous (but the word is often used in a vaguer sense, as it seems to be here).   20 *Renowmed* renowned.   21 *ruinous* decayed.   22 *earnestly* attentively. 23 *wasted* ruined.   26 *controll'd* rebuked.   27 *tawny* dark-complexioned. *dam* mother.   28 *bewray* betray, reveal.   *brat* child. The term was not so derogative as in modern usage.   29 *look* face (colour).   33 *rates* berates, rebukes.   36 *hold thee dearly* value you highly.   38 *Surpris'd* captured. *suddenly* quickly.   39 *To use . . . the man* to be dealt with as you think the man deserves.   42 *the pearl*

	This growing image of thy fiendlike face?	45
	Why dost not speak? What, deaf? not a word?	
	A halter, soldiers! Hang him on this tree,	
	And by his side his fruit of bastardy.	

AAR.   Touch not the boy! He is of royal blood.

LUC.   Too like the sire for ever being good.   50
       First hang the child, that he may see it sprawl—
       A sight to vex the father's soul withal.
       Get me a ladder.

> [*A ladder brought, which* Aaron *is
> made to climb.*]

ARR.   Lucius, save the child
       And bear it from me to the Emperess.
       If thou do this, I'll show thee wondrous things   55
       That highly may advantage thee to hear;
       If thou wilt not, befall what may befall,
       I'll speak no more — but vengeance rot you all!

LUC.   Say on; and if it please me which thou speak'st,
       Thy child shall live, and I will see it nourish'd.   60

AAR.   And if it please thee? Why, assure thee, Lucius,
       'Twill vex thy soul to hear what I shall speak;
       For I must talk of murders, rapes, and massacres,
       Acts of black night, abominable deeds,
       Complots of mischief, treason, villainies   65
       Ruthful to hear, yet piteously perform'd;
       And this shall all be buried in my death
       Unless thou swear to me my child shall live.

LUC.   Tell on thy mind. I say thy child shall live.

. . . *eye* An old proverb says that "A black man is a pearl in a fair woman's eye."
Blackness was regarded as a sign of a lustful disposition.   44 *wall-ey'd* fiercely
glaring; literally, with a discoloured iris which gives the eye a look of ferocity.   51
sprawl struggle in the agony of death.   52 *withal* with.   56 *highly may advantage thee* may be to your great advantage.   57 *befall . . . befall* let come what
may.   59 *if it . . . speak'st* if I like what you say.   60 *nourish'd* taken care of.
65 *Complots* plots.   66 *Ruthful* pitiful.   *piteously* so as to arouse pity.

AAR.	Swear that he shall, and then I will begin.	70
LUC.	Who should I swear by? Thou believest no god.	
	That granted, how canst thou believe an oath?	
AAR.	What if I do not? as indeed I do not.	
	Yet, for I know thou art religious	
	And hast a thing within thee called conscience,	75
	With twenty popish tricks and ceremonies	
	Which I have seen thee careful to observe,	
	Therefore I urge thy oath. For that I know	
	An idiot holds his bauble for a god	
	And keeps the oath which by that god he swears,	80
	To that I'll urge him. Therefore thou shalt vow	
	By that same god, what god soe'er it be,	
	That thou adorest and hast in reverence,	
	To save my boy, to nourish and bring him up,	
	Or else I will discover naught to thee.	85
LUC.	Even by my god I swear to thee I will.	
AAR.	First know thou, I begot him on the Empress.	
LUC.	O most insatiate and luxurious woman!	
AAR.	Tut, Lucius, this was but a deed of charity	
	To that which thou shalt hear of me anon.	90
	'Twas her two sons that murdered Bassianus;	
	They cut thy sister's tongue, and ravish'd her,	
	And cut her hands, and trimm'd her as thou sawest.	
LUC.	O detestable villain! call'st thou that trimming?	
AAR.	Why, she was wash'd and cut and trimm'd, and 'twas	95
	Trim sport for them which had the doing of it.	
LUC.	O barbarous beastly villains like thyself!	
AAR.	Indeed I was their tutor to instruct them.	

74 *for* because. 78 *urge* insist upon. *For that* because. 79 *bauble* stick with a
head at the end carried by a jester. 85 *discover* reveal. 88 *luxurious* lecherous.
90 *To* compared with. 96 *Trim* neat. 97 *barbarous* Used with a possible pun.
99 *codding* lustful. "Cod" means "testicle." 100 *set* game. 102 *fought at head*
Bulldogs, noted for their courage, would seize a bull by the nose. 104 *train'd*
led, enticed. *guileful* deceptive. 111 *cheater* (a) cheat, swindler (b) escheater,

That codding spirit had they from their mother,
As sure a card as ever won the set.   100
That bloody mind I think they learn'd of me,
As true a dog as ever fought at head.
Well, let my deeds be witness of my worth.
I train'd thy brethren to that guileful hole
Where the dead corpse of Bassianus lay.   105
I wrote the letter that thy father found
And hid the gold within that letter mention'd,
Confederate with the Queen and her two sons;
And what not done, that thou hast cause to rue,
Wherein I had no stroke of mischief in it?   110
I play'd the cheater for thy father's hand,
And when I had it, drew myself apart
And almost broke my heart with extreme laughter.
I pried me through the crevice of a wall
When for his hand he had his two sons' heads,   115
Beheld his tears, and laugh'd so heartily
That both mine eyes were rainy like to his;
And when I told the Empress of this sport,
She sounded almost at my pleasing tale
And for my tidings gave me twenty kisses.   120

GOTH.   What, canst thou say all this and never blush?

AAR.   Ay, like a black dog, as the saying is.

LUC.   Art thou not sorry for these heinous deeds?

AAR.   Ay, that I had not done a thousand more.
        Even now I curse the day (and yet I think   125
        Few come within the compass of my curse)
        Wherein I did not some notorious ill:
        As kill a man, or else devise his death;
        Ravish a maid, or plot the way to do it;

---

an officer who looked after the king's escheats (estates forfeited to the crown) and
thus would have plenty of opportunity for fraudulent activity.   112 *drew myself
apart* secluded myself.   114 *pried me* spied.   119 *sounded* fainted.   122 *like a
black dog* To blush like a black dog is a proverbial expression for not to blush
at all.

Accuse some innocent, and forswear myself;   130
Set deadly enmity between two friends;
Make poor men's cattle break their necks;
Set fire on barns and haystalks in the night
And bid the owners quench them with their tears.
Oft have I digg'd up dead men from their graves   135
And set them upright at their dear friends' door
Even when their sorrow almost was forgot,
And on their skins, as on the bark of trees,
Have with my knife carved in Roman letters
"Let not your sorrow die, though I am dead."   140
Tut, I have done a thousand dreadful things
As willingly as one would kill a fly;
And nothing grieves me heartily indeed
But that I cannot do ten thousand more.

LUC.   Bring down the devil, for he must not die   145
So sweet a death as hanging presently.

               [Aaron *is brought down from the lad-
               der.*]

AAR.   If there be devils, would I were a devil,
To live and burn in everlasting fire,
So I might have your company in hell
But to torment you with my bitter tongue!   150

LUC.   Sirs, stop his mouth and let him speak no more.

               Enter Æmilius.

GOTH.   My lord, there is a messenger from Rome
Desires to be admitted to your presence.

LUC.   Let him come near.
Welcome, Æmilius. What's the news from Rome?   155

ÆMIL.   Lord Lucius, and you princes of the Goths,
The Roman Emperor greets you all by me;

---

130 *forswear* perjure.   133 *haystalks* A dialectal form still sometimes encountered in England (Q¹; Q², κ: "haystakes").   135–6 *Oft have . . . friends' door* Shakespeare may have had in mind exactly such an episode which occurs in IV.II. of Christopher Marlowe's THE JEW OF MALTA.   141 *Tut* Q²; Q¹: "But."   146 *hanging*

And, for he understands you are in arms,
He craves a parley at your father's house,
Willing you to demand your hostages,   160
And they shall be immediately deliver'd.

GOTH.   What says our general?

LUC.   Æmilius, let the Emperor give his pledges
Unto my father and my uncle Marcus,
And we will come. — March, away!   *Flourish. Exeunt.* 165

◇◇◇◇◇◇◇◇◇◇◇◇◇◇

[SCENE II. *Rome. Before the house of* Titus.]

Enter Tamora *and her two* Sons, [Demetrius *and*
Chiron,] *disguised.*

TAM.   Thus, in this strange and sad habiliament,
I will encounter with Andronicus
And say I am Revenge, sent from below
To join with him and right his heinous wrongs.
Knock at his study, where they say he keeps   5
To ruminate strange plots of dire revenge.
Tell him Revenge is come to join with him
And work confusion on his enemies.

They knock, and Titus *opens his study
door* [*above*].

TIT.   Who doth molest my contemplation?
Is it your trick to make me ope the door,   10
That so my sad decrees may fly away
And all my study be to no effect?
You are deceiv'd; for what I mean to do

---

presently immediate hanging.   149 *So* provided that.   158 *for* because.   159
craves a parley requests a conference. 160 *demand* request.

    V.II. 1 *sad habiliament* dismal clothing.   5 *keeps* resides.   10 *ope* open.   11
sad decrees serious decisions. 12 *to no effect* useless.

See here in bloody lines I have set down;
And what is written shall be executed.   15

TAM.   Titus, I am come to talk with thee.

TIT.   No, not a word! How can I grace my talk,
         Wanting a hand to give it that accord?
         Thou hast the odds of me; therefore no more!

TAM.   If thou didst know me, thou wouldst talk with me.   20

TIT.   I am not mad; I know thee well enough.
         Witness this wretched stump, witness these crimson lines,
         Witness these trenches made by grief and care,
         Witness the tiring day and heavy night,
         Witness all sorrow, that I know thee well   25
         For our proud Empress, mighty Tamora!
         Is not thy coming for my other hand?

TAM.   Know, thou sad man, I am not Tamora;
         She is thy enemy, and I thy friend.
         I am Revenge, sent from th' infernal kingdom   30
         To ease the gnawing vulture of thy mind
         By working wreakful vengeance on thy foes.
         Come down and welcome me to this world's light;
         Confer with me of murder and of death.
         There's not a hollow cave or lurking place,   35
         No vast obscurity or misty vale,
         Where bloody murder or detested rape
         Can couch for fear, but I will find them out
         And in their ears tell them my dreadful name —
         Revenge, which makes the foul offender quake.   40

TIT.   Art thou Revenge? and art thou sent to me
         To be a torment to mine enemies?

---

17 *grace* make pleasing.   18 *Wanting* lacking.   *give . . . accord* accompany it
with a gesture, as an actor might do (POPE; Q¹: "giue that accord"; F¹: "giue it
action").   19 *the odds of* an advantage over.   23 *trenches* wrinkles.   24 *heavy*
(a) sorrowful (b) sleepy.   31 *To ease . . . mind* The image is drawn from the
story of Prometheus whose liver was gnawed by vultures.   32 *wreakful* avenging.
38 *couch* crouch stealthily.   *find them out* detect them.   46 *surance* assurance.
49 *globe* CAPELL; QQ, F¹: "globes."   50 *proper palfreys* handsome horses.   51 *hale*

TAM.   I am; therefore come down and welcome me.

TIT.   Do me some service ere I come to thee.
         Lo, by thy side where Rape and Murder stands,   45
         Now give some surance that thou art Revenge —
         Stab them, or tear them on thy chariot wheels;
         And then I'll come and be thy wagoner
         And whirl along with thee about the globe.
         Provide thee two proper palfreys, black as jet,   50
         To hale thy vengeful wagon swift away
         And find out murderers in their guilty caves;
         And when thy car is loaden with their heads,
         I will dismount, and by thy wagon wheel
         Trot like a servile footman all day long,   55
         Even from Hyperion's rising in the East
         Until his very downfall in the sea;
         And day by day I'll do this heavy task,
         So thou destroy Rapine and Murder there.

TAM.   These are my ministers and come with me.   60

TIT.   Are these thy ministers? What are they call'd?

TAM.   Rape and Murder; therefore called so
         'Cause they take vengeance of such kind of men.

TIT.   Good Lord, how like the Empress' sons they are!
         And you the Empress! But we worldly men   65
         Have miserable, mad, mistaking eyes.
         O sweet Revenge, now do I come to thee;
         And, if one arm's embracement will content thee,
         I will embrace thee in it by-and-by.   [*Exit above.*]

TAM.   This closing with him fits his lunacy.   70
         Whate'er I forge to feed his brainsick humours

---

draw.   52 *murderers* CAPELL; Q¹: "murder." *caves* CAPELL; Q¹: "cares." 53 *car*
chariot. *loaden* laden. 56 *Hyperion's* the sun god's (F²; QQ: "Epeons"; F¹: "Ep-
tons"). 57 *downfall* setting. 59 *So* provided that. 61 *these* DYCE; QQ, F¹: "them."
62 *Rape* Q¹; F², K: "Rapine." 63 *take . . . men* take such kinds of vengeance
upon men. 65 *worldly* mortal, of this world (Q²; Q¹: "wordlie"). 68 *one arm's
embracement* an embrace by one arm. 70 *closing with him* (a) embracing him
(b) agreeing with him. 71 *forge* invent. *humours* whims.

Do you uphold and maintain in your speeches,
For now he firmly takes me for Revenge;
And, being credulous in this mad thought,
I'll make him send for Lucius his son,   75
And whilst I at a banquet hold him sure,
I'll find some cunning practice out of hand
To scatter and disperse the giddy Goths,
Or at the least make them his enemies.
See, here he comes, and I must ply my theme.   80

[*Enter* Titus, *below.*]

TIT.   Long have I been forlorn, and all for thee.
         Welcome, dread Fury, to my woeful house.
         Rapine and Murder, you are welcome too.
         How like the Empress and her sons you are!
         Well are you fitted, had you but a Moor.   85
         Could not all hell afford you such a devil?
         For well I wot the Empress never wags
         But in her company there is a Moor;
         And, would you represent our queen aright,
         It were convenient you had such a devil.   90
         But welcome as you are. What shall we do?

TAM.   What wouldst thou have us do, Andronicus?

DEM.   Show me a murderer, I'll deal with him.

CHI.   Show me a villain that hath done a rape.
         And I am sent to be reveng'd on him.   95

TAM.   Show me a thousand that hath done thee wrong,
         And I will be revenged on them all.

TIT.   Look round about the wicked streets of Rome,
         And when thou find'st a man that's like thyself,
         Good Murder, stab him; he's a murderer.   100
         Go thou with him, and when it is thy hap
         To find another that is like to thee.

---

72 *uphold and maintain* support and carry on.   77 *practice* scheme.   *out of hand*
on the spur of the moment.   78 *giddy* foolish.   87 *wot* know.   *wags* goes about.
89 *would you . . . aright* if you would represent our queen properly.   90 *con-*
venient proper.   96 *hath* Q¹; Q², K: "haue."   101 *hap* chance.   106 *proportion*

Good Rapine, stab him; he's a ravisher.
Go thou with them; and in the Emperor's court
There is a queen, attended by a Moor.   105
Well shalt thou know her by thine own proportion,
For up and down she doth resemble thee.
I pray thee do on them some violent death;
They have been violent to me and mine.

TAM.   Well hast thou lesson'd us; this shall we do.   110
But would it please thee, good Andronicus,
To send for Lucius, thy thrice-valiant son,
Who leads towards Rome a band of warlike Goths,
And bid him come and banquet at thy house —
When he is here, even at thy solemn feast,   115
I will bring in the Empress and her sons,
The Emperor himself, and all thy foes;
And at thy mercy shall they stoop and kneel,
And on them shalt thou ease thy angry heart.
What says Andronicus to this device?   120

TIT.   Marcus, my brother! 'Tis sad Titus calls.

Enter Marcus.

Go, gentle Marcus, to thy nephew Lucius;
Thou shalt inquire him out among the Goths.
Bid him repair to me and bring with him
Some of the chiefest princes of the Goths.   125
Bid him encamp his soldiers where they are.
Tell him the Emperor and the Empress too
Feast at my house, and he shall feast with them.
This do thou for my love; and so let him,
As he regards his aged father's life.   130

MARC.   This will I do and soon return again.   [*Exit.*]

TAM.   Now will I hence about thy business
And take my ministers along with me.

---

shape, appearance.   107 *up and down* exactly.   110 *lesson'd* instructed.   115
solemn ceremonial.   120 *device* plan.   122 *gentle* noble.   124 *repair* come.   130
regards has concern for.

TIT.   Nay, nay! Let Rape and Murder stay with me;
        Or else I'll call my brother back again   135
        And cleave to no revenge but Lucius.

TAM.   [*aside to her sons*] What say you, boys? Will you abide
            with him
        Whiles I go tell my lord the Emperor
        How I have govern'd our determin'd jest?
        Yield to his humour, smooth and speak him fair,   140
        And tarry with him till I turn again.

TIT.   [*aside*] I knew them all, though they suppos'd me mad,
        And will o'erreach them in their own devices —
        A pair of cursed hellhounds and their dam!

DEM.   Madam, depart at pleasure; leave us here.   145

TAM.   Farewell, Andronicus. Revenge now goes
        To lay a complot to betray thy foes.

TIT.   I know thou dost; and, sweet Revenge, farewell.

                                    [*Exit* Tamora.]

CHI.   Tell us, old man, how shall we be employ'd?

TIT.   Tut, I have work enough for you to do.   150
        Publius, come hither! Caius and Valentine!

                [*Enter* Publius, Caius, *and* Valentine.]

PUB.   What is your will?

TIT.   Know you these two?

PUB.   The Empress' sons
        I take them — Chiron and Demetrius.   155

TIT.   Fie, Publius, fie! thou art too much deceiv'd.
        The one is Murder, Rape is the other's name;
        And therefore bind them, gentle Publius —
        Caius and Valentine, lay hands on them.
        Oft have you heard me wish for such an hour,   160

---

139 *govern'd . . . jest* managed the jest we had determined on.   140 *humour*
whim.   *smooth* flatter.   *speak him fair* use kindly language with him.   141 *turn
again* return.   143 *o'erreach . . . devices* outwit them in their own stratagems.
144 *dam* Q²; Q¹: "dame."   147 *lay a complot* arrange a plot.   155 *take them*

And now I find it. Therefore bind them sure,
And stop their mouths if they begin to cry.   [*Exit.*]

        [*They lay hold on* Chiron *and* De-
        metrius.]

CHI.   Villains, forbear! We are the Empress' sons.

PUB.   And therefore do we what we are commanded.
Stop close their mouths; let them not speak a word.   165
Is he sure bound? Look that you bind them fast.

        Enter Titus Andronicus *with a knife,*
        and Lavinia *with a basin.*

TIT.   Come, come, Lavinia! Look, thy foes are bound.
Sirs, stop their mouths, let them not speak to me;
But let them hear what fearful words I utter.
O villains, Chiron and Demetrius!   170
Here stands the spring whom you have stain'd with mud,
This goodly summer with your winter mix'd.
You kill'd her husband; and for that vile fault
Two of her brothers were condemn'd to death,
My hand cut off and made a merry jest;   175
Both her sweet hands, her tongue — and that more dear
Than hands or tongue, her spotless chastity,
Inhuman traitors, you constrain'd and forc'd.
What would you say if I should let you speak?
Villains, for shame you could not beg for grace.   180
Hark, wretches, how I mean to martyr you.
This one hand yet is left to cut your throats
Whiles that Lavinia 'tween her stumps doth hold
The basin that receives your guilty blood.
You know your mother means to feast with me,   185
And calls herself Revenge, and thinks me mad.
Hark, villains! I will grind your bones to dust,
And with your blood and it I'll make a paste;
And of the paste a coffin I will rear,

recognize them to be. *and* THEOBALD; not in QQ, F¹. 161 *sure* securely.   181
martyr mutilate. 183 *Whiles that* while. 189 *coffin* pie crust. This was the
usual word, without any necessarily sinister implications. *rear* make.

And make two pasties of your shameful heads,   190
And bid that strumpet, your unhallowed dam,
Like to the earth, swallow her own increase.
This is the feast that I have bid her to,
And this the banquet she shall surfeit on;
For worse than Philomel you us'd my daughter,   195
And worse than Progne I will be reveng'd.
And now prepare your throats. Lavinia, come,
Receive the blood; and when that they are dead,
Let me go grind their bones to powder small
And with this hateful liquor temper it;   200
And in that paste let their vile heads be bak'd.
Come, come, be every one officious
To make this banquet, which I wish may prove
More stern and bloody than the Centaurs' feast.

He cuts their throats.

So!   205
Now bring them in, for I will play the cook
And see them ready against their mother comes.

Exeunt [with the dead bodies].

❖❖❖❖❖❖❖❖❖❖❖❖❖❖

[SCENE III. *Court of* Titus' *house.*]

Enter Lucius, Marcus, *and the* Goths, [with Aaron *prisoner, and his* Child *in the arms of an* Attendant].

LUC.   Uncle Marcus, since it is my father's mind

---

190 *pasties* pies.   192 *Like to . . . own increase* swallow her own children, as the earth receives its children when they are buried.   194 *surfeit* overeat.   195–6 *Philomel . . . Progne* See Introduction, xiv.   200 *temper* blend.   202 *officious* busy.   204 *Centaurs' feast* When the Centaurs (creatures half man and half horse) were invited to the marriage feast of Hippodamia and Pirithous, King of the Lapithae, they tried to carry off the bride and the other women guests. A savage battle ensued. Shakespeare probably read the story in Ovid's METAMORPHOSES, Book XII.   207 *against* in preparation for the time when.

That I repair to Rome, I am content.

GOTH.   And ours with thine, befall what fortune will.

LUC.   Good uncle, take you in this barbarous Moor,
This ravenous tiger, this accursed devil.   5
Let him receive no sust'nance, fetter him,
Till he be brought unto the Empress' face
For testimony of her foul proceedings.
And see the ambush of our friends be strong;
I fear the Emperor means no good to us.   . 10

AAR.   Some devil whisper curses in mine ear
And prompt me that my tongue may utter forth
The venomous malice of my swelling heart!

LUC.   Away, inhuman dog, unhallowed slave!
Sirs, help our uncle to convey him in.   15

[*Exeunt some* Goths, *with* Aaron.] *Flourish*

The trumpets show the Emperor is at hand.

Sound trumpets. Enter Emperor *and*
Empress, *with* [Æmilius,] Tribunes,
[Senators,] *and others.*

SAT.   What, hath the firmament moe suns than one?

LUC.   What boots it thee to call thyself a sun?

MARC.   Rome's Emperor, and nephew, break the parle;
These quarrels must be quietly debated.   20
The feast is ready which the careful Titus
Hath ordain'd to an honourable end —
For peace, for love, for league, and good to Rome.
Please you therefore draw nigh and take your places.

V.III. 2 *repair* return.   3 *ours with thine* our men with yours.   9 *ambush*
hidden following (so as to avoid an ambush).   11 *mine* Q²; Q¹: "my."   17 *What
. . . than one* Lucius has assumed the manner of an emperor. That the king on
earth was analagous to the sun in heaven was a Renaissance commonplace. *firmament* heavens.   *moe* more (not a contraction, but a separate formation from the
same root).   18 *boots* avails.   19 *break the parle* interrupt the conference.   21
careful full of cares, sorrowful.   24 *Please you* may it please you to.

| SAT. | Marcus, we will. | 25 |

A table brought in. [The company sit.]
Trumpets sounding, enter Titus *like a*
Cook, placing the dishes, and Lavinia
with a veil over her face; [also Young
Lucius *and others].*

TIT.   Welcome, my lord; welcome, dread Queen;
       Welcome, ye warlike Goths; welcome, Lucius;
       And welcome all. Although the cheer be poor,
       'Twill fill your stomachs. Please you eat of it.

SAT.   Why art thou thus attir'd, Andronicus?   30

TIT.   Because I would be sure to have all well
       To entertain your Highness and your Empress.

TAM.   We are beholding to you, good Andronicus.

TIT.   An if your Highness knew my heart, you were.
       My lord the Emperor, resolve me this: 35
       Was it well done of rash Virginius
       To slay his daughter with his own right hand,
       Because she was enforc'd, stain'd, and deflow'r'd?

SAT.   It was, Andronicus.

TIT.   Your reason, mighty lord?   40

SAT.   Because the girl should not survive her shame,
       And by her presence still renew his sorrows.

TIT.   A reason mighty, strong, and effectual;
       A pattern, precedent, and lively warrant
       For me (most wretched) to perform the like.   45
       Die, die, Lavinia, and thy shame with thee!

---

26 *my lord* Q¹; Q², κ: "my gracious lord." *dread* awesome, royal.   28 *cheer* food.
33 *beholding* indebted.   34 *were* would be.   35 *resolve me this* answer this question for me.   36 *rash Virginius* Virginius killed his daughter, Virginia, to prevent
her from being raped (enforc'd) by the wicked judge, Apius. The story is in Livy's
ROMAN HISTORY, III, 44–58, and in Chaucer's PHYSICIAN'S TALE, where Shakespeare
is likely to have read it, but why he got the story wrong here is difficult to explain.
42 *still* continually.   44 *lively* striking.   *warrant* justification.   48 *unkind* un-

And with thy shame thy father's sorrow die!

He kills her.

SAT.   What hast thou done, unnatural and unkind?

TIT.   Kill'd her for whom my tears have made me blind.
        I am as woeful as Virginius was,   50
        And have a thousand times more cause than he
        To do this outrage; and it now is done.

SAT.   What, was she ravish'd? Tell who did the deed.

TIT.   Will 't please you eat? Will 't please your Highness feed?

TAM.   Why hast thou slain thine only daughter thus?   55

TIT.   Not I! 'Twas Chiron and Demetrius.
        They ravish'd her and cut away her tongue;
        And they, 'twas they, that did her all this wrong.

SAT.   Go fetch them hither to us presently.

TIT.   Why, there they are both, baked in this pie,   60
        Whereof their mother daintily hath fed,
        Eating the flesh that she herself hath bred.
        'Tis true, 'tis true! Witness my knive's sharp point!

He stabs the Empress.

SAT.   Die, frantic wretch, for this accursed deed!

[*He stabs* Titus.]

LUC.   Can the son's eye behold his father bleed?   65
        There's meed for meed, death for a deadly deed!

[*He stabs* Saturninus. *A great tumult.*
Lucius, Marcus, *and their Friends go
up into a gallery.*]

MARC.   You sad-fac'd men, people and sons of Rome,

---

natural, cruel.   51–2 *And have . . . this outrage* The crime against Titus is
greater than that against Virginius whose daughter was never actually raped.
This, in contradiction to lines 36–8, seems to indicate that Shakespeare knew the
true story of Apius and Virginia. The discrepancy is difficult to account for.   59
presently at once.   60 *this pie* Q¹; Q², κ: "that pie."   66 *meed for meed* measure
for measure.

By uproar sever'd, as a flight of fowl
Scatt'red by winds and high tempestuous gusts,
O, let me teach you how to knit again   70
This scattered corn into one mutual sheaf,
These broken limbs again into one body;
Lest Rome herself be bane unto herself,
And she whom mighty kingdoms curtsy to,
Like a forlorn and desperate castaway,   75
Do shameful execution on herself.
But if my frosty signs and chaps of age,
Grave witnesses of true experience,
Cannot induce you to attend my words,
[*To* Lucius] Speak, Rome's dear friend, as erst our an-
           cestor,   80
When with his solemn tongue he did discourse
To lovesick Dido's sad-attending ear
The story of that baleful burning night
When subtile Greeks surpris'd King Priam's Troy.
Tell us what Sinon hath bewitch'd our ears,   85
Or who hath brought the fatal engine in
That gives our Troy, our Rome, the civil wound.
My heart is not compact of flint nor steel;
Nor can I utter all our bitter grief,
But floods of tears will drown my oratory   90
And break my utt'rance, even in the time
When it should move ye to attend me most,
And force you to commiseration.
Here's Rome's young captain; let him tell the tale,
While I stand by and weep to hear him speak.   95

LUC.   Then, gracious auditory, be it known to you

---

68 *uproar* F²; QQ, F¹: "uproars." *sever'd* separated, scattered.   70 *knit again* re-
bind.   71 *corn* stalks of grain.   *mutual* united.   73 *Lest Rome* CAPELL; Q¹: "Let
Rome," preceded by the speech prefix, "Romane Lord." F¹ gives the speech to a
"Goth."   *bane* destruction.   74 *curtsy* bow in reverence.   76 *Do . . . herself*
commit suicide.   77 *frosty signs* white hair.   *chaps* wrinkles (literally, cracks in
the skin).   79 *attend* listen to.   80 *erst* formerly.   *our ancestor* i.e. Æneas.   82
sad-attending seriously listening.   83 *baleful* sorrowful.   84 *subtile* treacherous.
85 *Sinon* a Greek who persuaded the Trojans to bring the wooden horse within

That Chiron and the damn'd Demetrius
Were they that murdered our Emperor's brother,
And they it were that ravished our sister.
For their fell faults our brothers were beheaded,   100
Our father's tears despis'd, and basely cozen'd
Of that true hand that fought Rome's quarrel out
And sent her enemies unto the grave.
Lastly, myself unkindly banished,
The gates shut on me, and turn'd weeping out   105
To beg relief among Rome's enemies;
Who drown'd their enmity in my true tears
And op'd their arms to embrace me as a friend.
I am the turned forth, be it known to you,
That have preserv'd her welfare in my blood   110
And from her bosom took the enemy's point,
Sheathing the steel in my advent'rous body.
Alas, you know I am no vaunter, I!
My scars can witness, dumb although they are,
That my report is just and full of truth.   115
But soft! methinks I do digress too much,
Citing my worthless praise. O, pardon me!
For when no friends are by, men praise themselves.

MARC.   Now is my turn to speak. Behold the child.

> [Points to the Child in the arms of an
> Attendant.]

Of this was Tamora delivered,   120
The issue of an irreligious Moor,
Chief architect and plotter of these woes.
The villain is alive in Titus' house,

---

their gates. His name was proverbial for treachery.   86 *fatal engine* deadly contrivance (the wooden horse).   88 *compact* composed.   91 *break my utt'rance* interrupt my speech.   92 *attend* listen to.   93 *commiseration* pity.   96 *auditory* audience.   100 *fell faults* cruel crimes.   101 *cozen'd* cheated.   104 *unkindly* unnaturally.   109 *turned forth* one who was exiled.   110 *in* with.   111 *point* sword.   112 *advent'rous* willing to assume risk.   113 *vaunter* boaster.   114 *witness* give evidence.   115 *just* accurate.   116 *soft* let me be silent.   117 *my worthless praise* praise to which I am not entitled.   121 *issue* progeny.

And as he is to witness, this is true.
Now judge what cause had Titus to revenge   125
These wrongs unspeakable, past patience,
Or more than any living man could bear.
Now you have heard the truth, what say you, Romans?
Have we done aught amiss? Show us wherein,
And, from the place where you behold us pleading,   130
The poor remainder of Andronici
Will hand in hand all headlong hurl ourselves
And on the ragged stones beat forth our souls
And make a mutual closure of our house.
Speak, Romans, speak! and if you say we shall,   135
Lo, hand in hand, Lucius and I will fall.

ÆMIL.   Come, come, thou reverent man of Rome,
And bring our Emperor gently in thy hand —
Lucius our Emperor; for well I know
The common voice do cry it shall be so.   140

ALL.   Lucius, all hail, Rome's royal Emperor!

MARC.   Go, go into old Titus' sorrowful house,
And hither hale that misbelieving Moor
To be adjudg'd some direful slaught'ring death,
As punishment for his most wicked life.   145

                        [*Exeunt some* Attendants.]

                        [Lucius, Marcus, *and the others de-
                        scend.*]

ALL.   Lucius, all hail, Rome's gracious governor!

LUC.   Thanks, gentle Romans. May I govern so
To heal Rome's harms and wipe away her woe!
But, gentle people, give me aim awhile,

---

124 *And . . . witness* QQ, F¹; THEOBALD, K: "Damn'd as he is, to witness." There
is no justification for the emendation, although it has been widely accepted.
125 *cause* F⁴; QQ, F¹: "course."   126 *patience* man's ability to endure.   128 *Now*
now that. *you have* Q²; Q¹: "haue you."   129 *aught amiss* anything wrong.   133
ragged rough. *souls* Q¹; Q², K: "braines."   134 *mutual closure* common end.
141 *Lucius . . . Emperor* CAPELL; QQ, F¹ give the line to Marcus.   143 *hale* drag.
144 *adjudg'd* sentenced to (F¹; Q¹: "adiudge").   146 *Lucius . . . governor*

For nature puts me to a heavy task. 150
Stand all aloof. But, uncle, draw you near
To shed obsequious tears upon this trunk.
O, take this warm kiss on thy pale cold lips,
These sorrowful drops upon thy bloodstain'd face,
The last true duties of thy noble son! 155

MARC. Tear for tear, and loving kiss for kiss,
Thy brother Marcus tenders on thy lips.
O, were the sum of these that I should pay
Countless and infinite, yet would I pay them!

LUC. Come hither, boy; come, come, and learn of us 160
To melt in showers. Thy grandsire lov'd thee well.
Many a time he danc'd thee on his knee,
Sung thee asleep, his loving breast thy pillow.
Many a story hath he told to thee,
And bid thee bear his pretty tales in mind 165
And talk of them when he was dead and gone.

MARC. How many thousand times hath these poor lips,
When they were living, warm'd themselves on thine!
O, now, sweet boy, give them their latest kiss!
Bid him farewell; commit him to the grave; 170
Do him that kindness, and take leave of him.

BOY. O grandsire, grandsire! ev'n with all my heart
Would I were dead, so you did live again!
O Lord, I cannot speak to him for weeping;
My tears will choke me if I ope my mouth. 175

[*Enter* Attendants *with* Aaron.]

ROMAN. You sad Andronici, have done with woes.
Give sentence on this execrable wretch

CAPELL; QQ, F¹ give the line to Marcus.   149 *give me aim* guide me in my direction. To "give aim," a term from archery, is to guide one's aim by telling him where the previous shot has fallen.   150 *puts . . . task* imposes a sorrowful duty upon me.   151 *aloof* side.   152 *obsequious* mourning.   154 *bloodstain'd* F³; Q¹: "blood slaine."   157 *tenders* offers.   159 *Countless* too many to be reckoned.   162 *danc'd* dandled.   167 *hath* Q¹; K: "have."   169 *latest* final.   171 *Do him* F¹; Q¹: "Doe them." *of him* F¹; Q¹: "of them."

That hath been breeder of these dire events.

LUC. Set him breast-deep in earth, and famish him.
There let him stand and rave and cry for food.   180
If any one relieves or pities him,
For the offence he dies. This is our doom.
Some stay to see him fast'ned in the earth.

AAR. Ah, why should wrath be mute and fury dumb?
I am no baby, I, that with base prayers   185
I should repent the evils I have done.
Ten thousand worse than ever yet I did
Would I perform if I might have my will.
If one good deed in all my life I did,
I do repent it from my very soul.   190

LUC. Some loving friends convey the Emperor hence
And give him burial in his fathers' grave.
My father and Lavinia shall forthwith
Be closed in our household's monument.
As for that ravenous tiger, Tamora,   195
No funeral rite, nor man in mourning weed,
No mournful bell shall ring her burial;
But throw her forth to beasts and birds to prey.
Her life was beastly and devoid of pity,
And being dead, let birds on her take pity!   200
See justice done on Aaron, that damn'd Moor,
By whom our heavy haps had their beginning.
Then, afterwards, to order well the state,
That like events may ne'er it ruinate!   *Exeunt.*

---

182 *doom* sentence.   192 *his fathers' grave* the vault of his ancestors.   194
closed enclosed, entombed. *monument* tomb.   196 *weed* garment (Q¹; Q², K:
"weeds").   198 *to prey* to be preyed upon (Q¹; F¹, K: "of prey").   202 *heavy
haps* sad misfortunes.   204 *ruinate* bring to ruin.